The 21 Tenets of

Biblical Femininity

by Jerry & Sheryl Ross

Transitioning Girls
Into Young Ladies

www.stayinthecastle.com

TABLE OF CONTENTS

INTRODUCTION

Biblical femininity has all but disappeared in our modern culture. Satan has systematically targeted the tenets of Biblical femininity, eliminating them one by one from our society. However, many Christian young ladies are turning their hearts to God, their backs to the world, and reclaiming their Biblical heritage.

The following Bible principles are a result of a study of what the Word of God has to say concerning "young woman/women", "damsels", "daughters" and "maidens". From this study flows twenty-one tenets of Biblical femininity.

For the purpose of this study, we are defining a young lady as a female between 12 and 30 years of age.

Jerry & Sheryl Ross
August, 2012

3

Dedicated to our mothers,
Beverly Whittington and Donna Ross,
rubies both.

Young lady: defined as a female
between 12 and 30 years of age.

All Scripture from the King James Bible.

Printed in the United States of America.

Tenet 1

A young lady must choose between being a daughter of God, or a daughter of the world.

A Bible study on the subject of "young ladies" yields a first, great, and overwhelming truth — every young lady will at some point make a choice as to whose daughter she will be. I am not talking about trading in your mom and dad! This is not a decision about our physical parents, but a decision concerning your spiritual parentage. The Bible draws a distinct line between the daughters of God and the daughters of this world. The first step toward Biblical femininity is a clear-cut decision to embrace as your heavenly Father, the God of the universe.

This choice begins with the decision to accept Jesus as your Savior. If you have never received the gift of eternal life, my prayer is that you would do that now. Biblical femininity begins with a new birth. It flows from the new nature that comes with salvation.

John 3:5   Jesus answered, Verily, verily, I say unto thee, Except a man be born of water and of the Spirit, he cannot enter into the kingdom of God.

John 3:16-17   For God so loved the world, that he gave his only begotten Son, that whosoever believeth in him should not perish, but have everlasting life. For God sent not his Son into the world to condemn the world; but that the world through him might be saved.

2 Corinthians 5:17   Therefore if any man be in Christ, he is a new creature: old things are passed away; behold, all things are become new.

Trying to achieve Biblical femininity without Christ as your Savior is an impossibility! More importantly, the decision to be saved changes your eternal destination. Again, if you have never been saved, my prayer is that you would come under Holy Spirit conviction over your sin, that you would feel the drawing of the Father, and realize that Jesus was the Son of God. I pray you would then understand that Jesus died for your sins, was buried and rose again, and that you can be saved by placing your faith and trust in Christ and Christ alone for eternal life.

Yes, the first step in choosing between being a daughter of God or a daughter of this world is choosing Christ as Savior. But for the Christian girl, the choice is not complete until you fully embrace the new relationship now available to you as a child of God.

What does it mean to be a daughter of God? How does it differ from being a daughter of this world? The Bible again and again contrasts the two.

The Example of Noah's Generation

*Genesis 6:1-6 And it came to pass, when men began to multiply on the face of the earth, and daughters were born unto them, That the **sons of God** saw the **daughters of men** that they were fair; and they took them wives of all which they chose. And the LORD said, My spirit shall not always strive with man, for that he also is flesh: yet his days shall be an hundred and twenty years....And God saw that the wickedness of man was great in the earth, and that every imagination of the thoughts of his heart was only evil continually. And it repented the LORD that he had made man on the earth, and it grieved him at his heart.*

Only two civilizations existed for most of the 1600 years before the flood. One civilization was the descendants of Seth (Adam & Eve's third son) and the other, the descendants of Cain (Adam & Eve's first son). Seth followed in the ways of the Lord and Cain "went out from the presence of the Lord." One civilization was godly, the other ungodly. The two civilizations grew till they began to interact. The "sons of God" mentioned in Genesis chapter six are the descendants of Seth; the "daughters of men," the descendants of Cain. When the young men from the godly group foolishly began to marry the young women who descended from Cain, the result was the moral destruction of both civilizations.

Young lady, who will you be? Will you spend your life as a daughter of God, or a daughter of Cain?

The Example of Rebekah

*Genesis 24:2-4 And Abraham said unto his eldest servant of his house, that ruled over all that he had, Put, I pray thee, thy hand under my thigh: And I will make thee swear by the LORD, the God of heaven, and the God of the earth, that thou shalt not take a wife unto my son of the **daughters of the Canaanites**, among whom I dwell: But thou shalt go unto my country, and to my kindred, and take a wife unto my son Isaac.*

When it came time for Abraham to find a bride for his son, Isaac, he insisted the bride come from godly descendants. The "daughters of the Canaanites" were worldly, pagan young women.

Again, there were two groups of young ladies — daughters of God and daughters of this world. Isaac, wisely, married Rebekah, a sweet, godly young lady.

The Example of Rebekah's Children

Genesis 26:34 –35 And Esau was forty years old when he took to wife Judith the daughter of Beeri the Hittite, and Bashemath the daughter of Elon the Hittite: Which were a grief of mind unto Isaac and to Rebekah.

*Genesis 27:46 - 28:2 And Rebekah said to Isaac, I am weary of my life because of the **daughters of Heth**: if Jacob take a wife of the **daughters of Heth**, such as these which are of the **daughters of the land**, what good shall my life do me?.*

*Genesis 36:2 Esau took his wives of the **daughters of Canaan...***

Isaac and Rebekah had twin boys, Esau and Jacob. When the boys grew to men, Esau chose two wives who were Hittites. The Hittite young ladies were daughters of this world — young ladies who were not raised to believe in Jehovah God. His decision was a grief to the hearts of his parents.

Jacob wisely chose a daughter of God, a young lady named Rachel. Both kinds of young ladies were available. They still are today. Which will you be?

The Example of Dinah

*Genesis 34:1-9 And Dinah the daughter of Leah, which she bare unto Jacob, went out to see **the daughters of the land**....And Hamor communed with them, saying, The soul of my son Shechem longeth for your daughter: I pray you give her him to wife. And make ye marriages with us, and give **your daughters** unto us, and take **our daughters** unto you.*

Jacob had twelve sons and one daughter. Dinah, a young lady reared to be a daughter of God, decides to go and "see the daughters of the land." Through them, she meets a worldly young man, and loses her purity.

Again, two groups are identified — the daughters of God and the daughters of the world.

The Example of Generations of Israelites

*Numbers 25:1 And Israel abode in Shittim, and the people began to commit whoredom with the **daughters of Moab**.*

*Judges 3:5-7 And the children of Israel dwelt among the Canaanites, Hittites, and Amorites, and Perizzites, and Hivites, and Jebusites: **And they took their daughters to be their wives, and gave their daughters to their sons, and served their gods**. And the children of*

Israel did evil in the sight of the LORD, and forgat the LORD their God, and served Baalim and the groves.

*Ezra 9:12 Now therefore give not **your daughters** unto their sons, neither take **their daughters** unto your sons, nor seek their peace or their wealth for ever: that ye may be strong, and eat the good of the land, and leave it for an inheritance to your children for ever.*

*Nehemiah 10:29-30 They clave to their brethren, their nobles, and entered into a curse, and into an oath, to walk in God's law, which was given by Moses the servant of God, and to observe and do all the commandments of the LORD our Lord, and his judgments and his statutes; And that we would not give **our daughters** unto the people of the land, nor take **their daughters** for our sons:*

Throughout Israel's history, we see times when these sons and daughters of God lost their separatist stand. The nation staggered morally whenever they decided to intermarry with heathen people. Every generation of Israelite young people had to decide whether they would conduct themselves as children of God, or follow the ways of the children of men.

The Example of Samson

*Judges 14:1-3 And Samson went down to Timnath, and saw a woman in Timnath of the daughters of the Philistines. And he came up, and told his father and his mother, and said, I have seen a woman in Timnath of **the daughters of the Philistines**: now therefore get her for me to wife. Then his father and his mother said unto him, Is there never a woman among **the daughters of thy brethren**, or among all my people, that thou goest to take a wife of the uncircumcised Philistines? And Samson said unto his father, Get her for me; for she pleaseth me well.*

Samson bypassed the godly young ladies available in his day, and decided instead to pursue ungodly young women. As a result, Samson's story is one of great physical strength, yet greater moral failures. Again, we see in the story both types of young ladies existed.

The New Testament Challenge

From the second generation of mankind, Cain went away from God but Seth, his brother, followed God. Since then, every generation has contained both young people committed to God, and young people careless toward God.

As a young lady, you too must choose. This is the starting place. The rest of this book means nothing, if you make the wrong choice. The world has always been awash with young ladies whose lives, actions, and attitudes undermine the moral and spiritual foundation of their culture. The young lady who decides to be the exception is priced, in God's eyes, above rubies! And because of her wise choice, she is graced to wear the title: daughter of God.

*2 Corinthians 6:14—7:1 Be ye not unequally yoked together with unbelievers: for what fellowship hath righteousness with unrighteousness? and what communion hath light with darkness? And what concord hath Christ with Belial? or what part hath he that believeth with an infidel? And what agreement hath the temple of God with idols? for ye are the temple of the living God; as God hath said, I will dwell in them, and walk in them; and I will be their God, and they shall be my people. Wherefore come out from among them, and be ye separate, saith the Lord, and touch not the unclean thing; and I will receive you, And will be a Father unto you, and **ye shall be my sons and daughters**, saith the Lord Almighty. Having therefore these promises, dearly beloved, let us cleanse ourselves from all filthiness of the flesh and spirit, perfecting holiness in the fear of God.*

Tenet 2

A young lady embraces the purpose of her creation.

Genesis 2:18   And the LORD God said, It is not good that the man should be alone; I will make him an help meet for him.

A godly young lady understands and embraces the purpose for which God created her. The first man and woman were not created at the same time, in the same way, or for the same purpose. The feminine woman wants, above all, to please the Lord. For this reason, she examines carefully her divine purpose.

Genesis 1:27   So God created man in his own image, in the image of God created he him; male and female created he them.

Genesis 2:7-8   And the LORD God formed man of the dust of the ground, and breathed into his nostrils the breath of life; and man became a living soul. And the LORD God planted a garden eastward in Eden; and there he put the man whom he had formed.

Genesis 2:18-25   And the LORD God said, It is not good that the man should be alone; I will make him an help meet for him...And the LORD God caused a deep sleep to fall upon Adam, and he slept: and he took one of his ribs, and closed up the flesh instead thereof; And the rib, which the LORD God had taken from man, made he a woman, and brought her unto the man. And Adam said, This is now bone of my bones, and flesh of my flesh: she shall be called Woman, because she was taken out of Man. Therefore shall a man leave his father and his mother, and shall cleave unto his wife: and they shall be one flesh. And they were both naked, the man and his wife, and were not ashamed.

Man was created first by God, formed by His hands from the dust of the earth, divinely gifted a living soul, placed in a garden, and given both responsibilities and rules.

Woman was created secondly by God, formed by His hands, fashioned around a rib taken out of the man, divinely gifted a living soul, and brought to the man for the purpose of being, for the man, a companion and helper.

Joined together by sacred matrimony, Woman was so named because she was taken out of Man as a gift to Man. Man was instructed to make his relationship to her the most important of all human relationships, and to faithfully cleave to her with the understanding that they were now one flesh.

The purpose of Adam was to accept the responsibilities and respect the rules that God had placed upon him. The purpose of Eve was to provide help and companionship to Adam so that he might better accomplish what God had created him to do.

Young lady, you were created to be a helper and companion to a young man whom God will bring to you in His time.

A Christian lady does not rebel against God's original intent, but instead embraces her divine purpose. Her femininity is defined by her passion in first preparing for, then carrying out the blessed calling of being both a helper and companion to the man God has given her.

Now the question — are you willing to embrace your divine intent? Young lady, are you preparing yourself so that in every way you will be a blessed help to a godly young man? Are you accepting of the fact that his life is not to be centered upon you, but focused on his responsibilities assigned to him by God? Are you prepared to lose yourself in helping him succeed in his life's calling? Is your life now characterized by selfless service or by serving self?

Daughters of the world despise this teaching. They sacrifice their femininity upon the altar of their selfish agenda and humanistic ideology. They fight to reverse divinely-appointed roles, and then wonder why their lives seem so empty, and their husbands so miserable.

Real ladies embrace God's divine intent — no, not just embrace it, they glory in it!

Tenet 3

A young lady prepares herself for the young man God has created for her to marry.

Genesis 2:21-24 And the LORD God caused a deep sleep to fall upon Adam, and he slept: and he took one of his ribs, and closed up the flesh instead thereof; And the rib, which the LORD God had taken from man, made he a woman, and brought her unto the man. And Adam said, This is now bone of my bones, and flesh of my flesh: she shall be called Woman, because she was taken out of Man. Therefore shall a man leave his father and his mother, and shall cleave unto his wife: and they shall be one flesh.

Every young lady dreams of one day being happily married. You want to find "Mr. Right." At times, you might question whether he is real. The Bible gives you the answer — an answer that I think will be an encouragement to you!

God has created someone specifically for you! This is one of the greatest of all Biblical truths. Eve was created as the perfect fit, the perfect complement to Adam. God made you to be someone's Eve. This is something you need to, by faith, believe! Somewhere, within a reasonable time frame of when you were born, a young baby boy was delivered. God formed you in your mother's womb to be his soul-mate, and him yours.

A part of that special young man already dwells within you. God created Eve from a rib taken from Adam. A part of the man she was created to complete was in her. I believe God does the same for every young lady. This is how carefully, how specifically, God has planned your future. Trust the Lord — your young man is out there!

You will never feel complete until you meet this person. The great mystery of marriage is this — how can two people become one?

God states that when two people marry, "they shall be one flesh." How can this be? Doesn't 1+1=2? How can 1+1=1? The answer is simple — neither you nor your young man are complete people, and you will not be until you are brought together. The frustration, the divine longing that every young lady struggles with, is a feeling of incompleteness. It is a desire to be whole.

Satan will bring to you a counterfeit before God brings to you His choice. Always! Satan has determined to counterfeit everything God has ever done. He will try to capitalize on your frustration.

God will bring the two of you together in His time. God caused a deep sleep to fall upon Adam until He brought Eve to Adam. God will do the same for you — in His time. Till then, let your heart sleep.

The world system works hard to convince young ladies that they must spend their lives pursuing young men until they find the one God made for them. Hollywood movies, romance novels, pop culture love songs, teen magazines, and an array of other worldly influences place a lot of pressure on young ladies to have a boyfriend. You have to make a choice on whether to trust God, and believe that He will bring you together, or to waste your precious young lady years riding the romance roller coaster, involving yourself in relationships never intended or sanctioned by God.

Your young lady years should be about preparation, not pursuit. For the young lady who has placed her trust in God concerning this decision, pursuit is not necessary. She can relax, wait, and prepare knowing that the Lord has this under control.

I never worry about the young lady who chooses not to have a boyfriend — to forgo all of that and wait for God's perfect will and perfect timing. I do worry about the young lady who *can't not* have a boyfriend.

Trust the Lord. The young man God has for you is out there. He is preparing for you. Your young lady years should be spent preparing for him. He is deserving of a young wife who is patient, pure, and prepared. You both have a wonderful life to live out together.

A real lady would be foolish to miss it!

Tenet 4

A young lady is the antithesis of the strange woman.

In order to achieve Biblical femininity, you need to be introduced to a Bible woman. A young lady needs to intimately understand this woman — to dissect her attributes and understand her mindset. Some people you study so that you can emulate them. This woman you will study so that you never become her. The female I am speaking of is known simply as the "strange woman."

*Proverbs 2:10-20 When wisdom entereth into thine heart, and knowledge is pleasant unto thy soul; Discretion shall preserve thee, understanding shall keep thee.....To deliver thee from **the strange woman**, even from the stranger which flattereth with her words; Which forsaketh the guide of her youth, and forgetteth the covenant of her God. For her house inclineth unto death, and her paths unto the dead. None that go unto her return again, neither take they hold of the paths of life. That thou mayest walk in the way of good men, and keep the paths of the righteous.*

Proverbs reveals distinct details concerning the strange woman. Wisdom, knowledge, discretion, and understanding guard you from following her path. In the above Scriptures, it is interesting to note that she was afforded a choice to become something other than what she is. Notice that, in her youth, she had a godly guide. At one time she could have entered into a covenant with her God. There was opportunity to choose a better path and to live by better principles. Instead, she forsook the guide of her youth and forgot the covenant of her God. In turning her back on what light God had provided for her, she chose instead to plunge down a dark path, away from Biblical femininity and toward devilish debauchery.

The seventh chapter of Proverbs affords us an eyewitness account of the strange woman at work — her personality, her purpose, and her perverseness.

Proverbs 7:1-7 My son, keep my words, and lay up my commandments with thee. Keep my commandments, and live; and my law as the apple of thine eye. Bind them upon thy fingers, write them upon the table of thine heart. Say unto wisdom, Thou art my sister; and call understanding thy kinswoman: That they may keep thee from the **strange woman,** *from the stranger which flattereth with her words. For at the window of my house I looked through my casement, And beheld among the simple ones, I discerned among the youths, a young man void of understanding, Passing through the street near her corner; and he went the way to her house...*

Attributes of the Strange Woman

1. The strange woman is a predator.

The young man in this chapter is identified as a one, "void of understanding." He is one of the "simple ones." This is who she targets for destruction.

The strange woman at one time made a choice to refuse a holy path and a godly lifestyle. Her misery now wants company. The first attribute of the strange woman is that she wants others to fall into the same shame and sin that now defines her. So she targets innocent young ladies and simple young men, seeking to influence them away from God.

Proverbs 23:27-28 For a whore is a deep ditch; and a strange woman is a narrow pit. She also lieth in wait as for a prey, and increaseth the transgressors among men.

2. The strange woman is a woman of the night.

Proverbs 7:8-9 Passing through the street near her corner; and he went the way to her house, In the twilight, in the evening, in the black and dark night:

The time of day of this seduction is well worth noting. One of the attributes of the strange woman is her enchantment with the dark hours.

The practical lesson for a young lady is this: night-time holds more danger and more risk of evil than the day-time hours. A wise young lady does not wander aimlessly after dark. She does not just "hang out." After dark, she is at home, at church, at work, or at a well-planned, well-chaperoned activity.

The spiritual lessons abound.

1 John 1:5-7 This then is the message which we have heard of him, and declare unto you, that God is light, and in him is no darkness at all. If we say that we have fellowship with him, and walk in darkness, we lie, and do not the truth: But if we walk in the light, as he is in the light, we have fellowship one with another, and the blood of Jesus Christ his Son cleanseth us from all sin.

1 Thessalonians 5:4-8 But ye, brethren, are not in darkness, that that day should overtake you as a thief. Ye are all the children of light, and the children of the day: we are not of the night, nor of darkness. Therefore let us not sleep, as do others; but let us watch and be sober. For they that sleep sleep in the night; and they that be drunken are drunken in the night. But let us, who are of the day, be sober, putting on the breastplate of faith and love; and for an helmet, the hope of salvation.

God is light! A young lady dedicated to adopting Biblical femininity seeks to walk in the light of God's Word. The Bible truly becomes a lamp unto her feet and a light unto her path. She lives as a child of the light — sober, alert, full of faith and love.

The strange woman seeks and embraces darkness, foolishly thinking that it hides her wickedness from observation. She fails to realize that God sees in the dark!

3. The strange woman dresses in the attire of a harlot.

Proverbs 7:10 And, behold, there met him a woman with the attire of an harlot, and subtle of heart.

Note it does not say she is a harlot (although, we certainly will observe she lacks moral character). What it does say is that she purposefully dresses to draw men's eyes to her body. Her attire advertises her disdain for chastity and purity, and suggests to men that she is open to seduction.

There is a HUGE difference in clothing that makes you look feminine and clothing that makes you look sexy. A Christian lady chooses carefully what she wears, selecting clothes that quiet her womanly form, making her look feminine, but not cheap. Skirts or dresses that are too tight or too short, tops that are too tight and too low, and form -fitting pants and shorts all send an unchaste and ungodly message.

Young lady, if you are going to be virtuous in your dress, then you are going to have to bypass most of the styles of this culture. At times this is frustrating! Shopping becomes a chore. The world has dedicated itself to providing a vast array of strange woman attire and very little that a discerning, dedicated Christian young lady can wear. This is no excuse to drop your standard. Femininity does not compromise in this area of life.

4. The strange woman possesses a subtle heart.
Proverbs 7:10   And, behold, there met him a woman....subtle of heart.

The word *subtle* means *concealed* or *hidden*. Within her heart she carries hidden motives. She is deceitful and deceptive. This makes her untrustworthy.

Femininity flows from a pure heart. Your motives and manner of life should be honest and honorable. Nothing dims the countenance, steals the smile, and pollutes preciousness like deceit. Be open and honest with people in your life. Be transparent toward your parents. Be open with your pastor. Be honest with yourself and your God.

5. The strange woman is loud.
Proverbs 7:11 (She is loud....)

The Hebrew word translated loud is defined thus: *be disquieted, loud, mourn, be moved, make a noise, rage, roar, sound, be troubled, make in tumult, tumultuous, be in an uproar*. Obviously, *loud* in this verse means much more than the volume of your voice.

A troubled, subtle heart boils over. The strange woman, laden with sin, most often tries to mask her misery with verbal bluster. Her heart is in turmoil, and from the abundance of her heart, her mouth speaks.

A pure heart produces sweet musings. Words flow from an uncumbered spirit, and bless those who hear. A feminine lady protects the purity of her heart, and the peace it produces anoints her words.

6. The strange woman is stubborn.

Proverbs 7:11 (She is loud and stubborn...)

1 Samuel 15:23 For rebellion is as the sin of witchcraft, and stubbornness is as iniquity and idolatry...

The strange woman turns stubbornly away from God's original intent for her life. She sets her course away from femininity and toward rebellion. Young lady, has stubbornness crept into your life?

God likens the sin of stubbornness to iniquity and idolatry. When a young lady — who was created by God to be a companion and helper to the young man God created for her — rejects that path, she makes an idol of her own will, and becomes a servant to this new false god.

Femininity yields sweetly and easily to the will of God. *Feminism* has influenced several generations to rebel against God's original intent and to stubbornly insist on making a god of oneself.

7. The strange woman disdains her home.

Proverbs 7:11-12 (...her feet abide not in her house: Now is she without, now in the streets, and lieth in wait at every corner.)

Home to the strange woman is seen as a prison — a place from which to escape whenever possible. To a godly lady, her home is a sanctuary — a safe refuge and a sacred responsibility.

Modern day feminism holds stay-at-home-moms in disdain. Worldly women rule the day-time air-waves, boasting of their liberalism and their supposed liberty. Yet a quick peek behind the curtain of their personal lives reveals failed marriages, dysfunctional children, and, many times, sexual perversions.

Bible-based femininity embraces the role God has created for a woman. Never let anyone hold you in disdain for desiring to be a good wife and a godly mother. Never trade in your calling for a career. Make your husband your hero, your home your palace, and your children your priority.

8. The strange woman is a shameless flirt.

Proverbs 7:13-15 So she caught him, and kissed him, and with an impudent face said unto him, I have peace offerings with me; this day have I payed my vows. Therefore came I forth to meet thee, diligently to seek thy face, and I have found thee.

Many a young lady in our culture is patterning her behavior toward young men after the example of the strange woman! It is improper to lay hands on a young man, to flirt and kiss. A godly young lady would do none of these things.

How you speak to young men and about young men reveals much about your heart! The strange woman speaks suggestively and seductively.

Proverbs 7:21 With her much fair speech she caused him to yield, with the flattering of her lips she forced him.

Proverbs 6:23-25 For the commandment is a lamp; and the law is light; and reproofs of instruction are the way of life: To keep thee from the evil woman, from the flattery of the tongue of a strange woman.

Proverbs 5:3-4 For the lips of a strange woman drop as an honeycomb, and her mouth is smoother than oil: But her end is bitter as wormwood, sharp as a twoedged sword.

As a godly young woman, you need to behave carefully around all men. Your propriety will preserve your virtue. It is fine to be guardedly friendly, but never forward or flirtatious toward men.

9. The strange woman has no respect for the marriage vows.

Proverbs 7:16-19 I have decked my bed with coverings of tapestry, with carved works, with fine linen of Egypt. I have perfumed my bed with myrrh, aloes, and cinnamon. Come, let us take our fill of love until the morning: let us solace ourselves with loves. For the goodman is not at home, he is gone a long journey:

Our society is overrun with worldly women who think nothing of destroying their own marriages, or someone else's marriage. A wedding ring used to mean "hands off," but to the strange woman, it is just the opposite — it is a challenge!

A Christian lady views marriage as honorable. She holds in high regard her wedding vows, and would do nothing to put at risk her marriage or that of another.

10. The strange woman rejoices in the destruction of the simple.

Proverbs 7:25-26 Let not thine heart decline to her ways, go not astray in her paths. For she hath cast down many wounded: yea, many strong men have been slain by her.

Once the strange woman has destroyed a man, she is done with him. She will eventually begin to target someone else. Her goal is to destroy "many." Destroying people becomes her perverted and pro-fane mission in life. Like a trophy hunter, she takes her prey, mounts their heads in her hall of shame, and goes out to hunt again.

No Christian lady would wish to live this type of life. True-hearted, God-blessed femininity holds in disdain the perverted ways of the strange woman.

In a real sense, the strange woman becomes a co-laborer of Satan.

Proverbs 5:5 Her feet go down to death; her steps take hold on hell.

The goal of femininity is to glorify God. The goal of the strange woman is to populate hell. The virtuous woman is an ally of God, the strange woman, an agent of Satan.

Now let's consider the biography of the strange woman:
- She turned her back on whatever light and spiritual opportunities she once had.
- She is a moral predator.
- She — both literally and figuratively — embraces the darkness.
- She dresses seductively.
- She speaks suggestively.
- She has a deceitful heart.
- She is loud and obnoxious.
- She is stubborn.
- She holds in contempt her responsibilities at home.

- She has no respect for the institution of marriage.
- She is a shameless flirt.
- She has given herself to the destruction of anyone simple or foolish enough to be influenced by her.
- She has allowed herself to become an agent of Satan.

EVERYTHING she is should be held in disdain by a Christian lady! Femininity takes note of her character traits, and determines to be just the opposite.

Consider carefully the attributes of the strange woman. In the next chapter, we will introduce to you the virtuous woman. Study both carefully, and determine which you will be.

Tenet 5

A young lady embraces the attributes of virtue.

2 Peter 1:2-3 Grace and peace be multiplied unto you through the knowledge of God, and of Jesus our Lord, According as his divine power hath given unto us all things that pertain unto life and godliness, through the knowledge of him that hath called us to glory and virtue:

*Proverbs 31:10 Who can find a **virtuous woman**? for her price is far above rubies.*

In contrast to the strange woman of Proverbs chapter 7 (the antithesis of femininity) is the virtuous woman of Proverbs chapter 31 (the role model of femininity).

God declares this sainted lady as rare as precious gems, and of much greater value. Rubies pale in comparison! She is the bejeweled cornerstone of both the blessed home and the blessed nation.

1. The virtuous woman is a wonderful, trustworthy companion to her husband.

Proverbs 31:11-12 The heart of her husband doth safely trust in her, so that he shall have no need of spoil. She will do him good and not evil all the days of her life.

The virtuous woman is wonderful because of her determination to be a blessing to her husband. She is trustworthy because she will never give her husband any reason to doubt her loyalty. She can be counted upon!

Young lady, you can choose to join the ranks of the fickle, flirtatious females of our day, or you can begin now to develop the virtues of loyalty and chastity. Save your heart for the person of God's choosing, then be good to him all the days of your life.

2. The virtuous woman is industrious.

Proverbs 31:13 She seeketh wool, and flax, and worketh willingly with her hands.

Proverbs 31:17 She girdeth her loins with strength, and strengtheneth her arms.

Proverbs 31:27 She looketh well to the ways of her household, and eateth not the bread of idleness.

Young lady, make no mistake — femininity is no excuse to avoid work. Just the opposite is true. A Christian lady heeds well the warnings found in the Bible against slothfulness. It is lady-like to jump in, roll up your sleeves and work! Always look for opportunities to serve.

3. The virtuous woman is financially wise.

Proverbs 31:14 She is like the merchants' ships; she bringeth her food from afar.

A merchant buys wholesale. He goes the extra distance to secure the best prices for quality goods. A young lady should learn to be a wise shopper. She must compare prices, seek out bargains, and search out the best deals.

Proverbs 31:16 She considereth a field, and buyeth it: with the fruit of her hands she planteth a vineyard.

The virtuous woman gardens. Instead of buying everything, she is willing to put in the work to raise fresh produce. For the price of a handful of seed, she stocks her cupboards with nourishing, home-grown fruits and vegetables.

Proverbs 31:18 She perceiveth that her merchandise is good: her candle goeth not out by night.

The cheapest choice is not always the best choice. The virtuous woman not only looks for a reasonable price, but also considers carefully the quality of the merchandise. What she buys must last, so she shops smart.

Proverbs 31:24 She maketh fine linen, and selleth it; and deliver-

eth girdles unto the merchant.

The virtuous woman is a stay-at-home entrepreneur. In addition to her bargain shopping, her gardening, and her wise purchases, she uses her home-making skills to earn an income. What a blessing to her household! Not only does she manage well her household budget, she finds a way to add to the family income.

4. The virtuous woman is well skilled in home-keeping.

Proverbs 31:15 She riseth also while it is yet night, and giveth meat to her household, and a portion to her maidens.

Proverbs 31:19 She layeth her hands to the spindle, and her hands hold the distaff.

Proverbs 31:22 She maketh herself coverings of tapestry; her clothing is silk and purple.

Proverbs 31:27 She looketh well to the ways of her household, and eateth not the bread of idleness.

Every young lady needs to develop the character and the skills that you will use daily as a wife and mother. Learn to cook nutritious, money-saving meals from "scratch." Learn to sew. Learn from your mother how to manage a family.

This virtuous woman looks well to the "ways of her household." Not only does she see to it that her husband is helped, she also manages the children, seeing to their individual needs.

This involves getting out of bed early! *"She riseth also while it is yet night."* Her day starts long before most people are stirring.

5. The virtuous woman is tender-hearted toward those in need.

Proverbs 31:20 She stretcheth out her hand to the poor; yea, she reacheth forth her hands to the needy.

A very Christ-like attribute for all of us to learn is that of helping those in need. Jesus never bypassed an opportunity to help someone less fortunate. We see that the virtuous woman is pro-active in seeking out opportunities to help others — she "stretcheth out her hand....she reacheth forth her hands..."

One of the greatest of all virtues to learn in your youth is that of compassionate care toward those who are truly in need. Look around your church and around your community for people who need a hand up! Be a friend to the friendless, and a provider to the poor. God blesses those who stop to bless others.

Proverbs 21:13 Whoso stoppeth his ears at the cry of the poor, he also shall cry himself, but shall not be heard.

6. The virtuous woman is modest and feminine in her attire.

Proverbs 31:22 She maketh herself coverings of tapestry; her clothing is silk and purple.

Again, virtue is contrasted with strangeness. We learned that the strange woman adorns herself with the "attire of an harlot" — clothes designed to expose her flesh and advertise her immoral leanings. Virtue chooses "coverings." She adorns herself modestly. She chooses the feminine fabrics of tapestry, silk and purple. Virtue dresses beautifully feminine, yet safely modest.

Young lady, the world will force you to choose. Don't buy into their "strange" definition of womanhood. Dress distinctively. Your clothes should be unapologetically gender-specific and unquestionably modest. Choose to be the exception — choose to be a lady!

7. The virtuous woman dedicates herself to making her husband a success.

Proverbs 31:23 Her husband is known in the gates, when he sitteth among the elders of the land.

Noted among her attributes is the stated fact of her husband's good reputation and godly stature. He is a respected and successful leader in his community. Much of this success he can attribute to his wife. She does her job so that he can focus on his. She also pitches in and helps him with what God has called him to do. Because of these things, she is a vital ingredient to his success.

(Note: I have often publicly stated that if you were to dust anything I have ever done that was successful, you would find my wife's fingerprints all over it. I have been blessed to marry a woman who has spent her life helping me to be successful in what God has called me to do. My wish for the young ladies who read this book is that you would choose to do the same for the man God

has for you. — Pastor Ross)

8. The virtuous woman has the strength to live by a code of honor.

Proverbs 31:25   Strength and honour are her clothing; and she shall rejoice in time to come.

Strength and honor — what a combination! This is her covering; this is her protection.

What produces femininity? The answer is simple: a code of honor. A lady lives by Bible principles, not baseless pressures. She is not swayed by the culture, the crowd, or carnality. The twenty-one tenets of femininity taught in the Word of God provide the basis of her code of honor. There are things she simply will not do, places she will not go, clothes she will not wear, and words she will not say. Period.

Femininity is not weak. It takes great resolve and incredible inner strength to live a godly life in this ungodly culture. Isn't it time to turn your back on peer pressure, and turn your face toward God? Live in His light, and seek first and foremost His approval. Make the twenty-one tenets in this book *your* code of honor, and refuse to compromise, no matter the consequences.

9. The virtuous woman is wise and kind with her words.

Proverbs 31:26   She openeth her mouth with wisdom; and in her tongue is the law of kindness.

Wisdom anoints her words. A godly lady passes laws concerning the use of her tongue. She remains silent if what she is tempted to say is unwise or unkind. With God's help, she learns to bridle her tongue, and by doing so, she achieves Christian maturity and self-discipline.

James 3:2 For in many things we offend all. If any man offend not in word, the same is a perfect man, and able also to bridle the whole body.

10. The virtuous woman is dedicated to the care of her family.

Proverbs 31:15   She riseth also while it is yet night, and giveth meat to her household, and a portion to her maidens.

Proverbs 31:21 She is not afraid of the snow for her household: for all her household are clothed with scarlet.

Proverbs 31:27-28 She looketh well to the ways of her household, and eateth not the bread of idleness. Her children arise up, and call her blessed; her husband also, and he praiseth her.

The success of her husband and the care of her children are priority one! A godly lady manages well the home, seeing to it that the needs of her family come first.

11. The virtuous woman fears the Lord.

Proverbs 31:30 Favour is deceitful, and beauty is vain: but a woman that feareth the LORD, she shall be praised.

Femininity lives in awe of God! A true Christian lady wishes to reflect in her life His holiness and His righteousness. Her reverential respect of God allows her to grow in knowledge, understanding and wisdom. It also shields her from foolishness.

Proverbs 1:7 The fear of the LORD is the beginning of knowledge: but fools despise wisdom and instruction.

Proverbs 9:10 The fear of the LORD is the beginning of wisdom: and the knowledge of the holy is understanding.

12. The virtuous woman will be honored and blessed!

Proverbs 31:28-31 Her children arise up, and call her blessed; her husband also, and he praiseth her. Many daughters have done virtuously, but thou excellest them all. Favour is deceitful, and beauty is vain: but a woman that feareth the LORD, she shall be praised. Give her of the fruit of her hands; and let her own works praise her in the gates.

The world may never understand, and the culture will shake its head in disapproval, but God sees and blesses the lady who chooses virtue! Her husband will praise her, and her children will rise up and call her blessed. In the end, to gain the approval of God is far better than the applause of a corrupt world!

How about it? Do you want your life to really mean something? Choose rubies over rubbish! Choose to be a virtuous lady.

Tenet 6

A young lady understands the value of hard work.

Femininity and hard work are not opposing notions. Quite the contrary is true! In the last chapter, we saw the virtuous woman as both active and industrious. A real lady never shirks work — instead she embraces opportunities to serve.

The Example of Rebekah

*Genesis 24:14-15,20 And let it come to pass, that **the damsel** to whom I shall say, Let down thy pitcher, I pray thee, that I may drink; and she shall say, Drink, and I will give thy camels drink also: let the same be she that thou hast appointed for thy servant Isaac; and thereby shall I know that thou hast showed kindness unto my master. And it came to pass, before he had done speaking, that, behold, Rebekah came out, who was born to Bethuel, son of Milcah, the wife of Nahor, Abraham's brother, with her pitcher upon her shoulder...And she hasted, and emptied her pitcher into the trough, and ran again unto the well to draw water, and drew for all his camels.*

Abraham sent his servant to find a wife for his son, Isaac. The servant asked the Lord to reveal who this special lady should be by a display of her willingness to serve. Rebekah came to draw water, and offered to draw extra for both Abraham's servant and his camels. This was work! One camel can drink 30 to 50 gallons at a time. The Bible tells us that Isaac's servant had taken ten camels on this journey. That is 300 to 500 gallons of water that Rebekah drew from the well that day! This Bible lady was not afraid of hard work.

The Example of Ruth

Ruth 2:5-7 Then said Boaz unto his servant that was set over the *reapers, Whose **damsel** is this? And the servant that was set over the reapers answered and said, It is the Moabitish **damsel** that came back with Naomi out of the country of Moab: And she said, I pray you, let me glean and gather after the reapers among the sheaves: so she came, and hath continued even from the morning until now, that she tarried a little in the house.*

The lady who was to become the great-great grandmother of King David earned her way into the heart of Boaz by her willingness to work hard to provide for both herself and her widowed mother-in-law. This gracious and godly Moabite woman spent the days of harvest, gleaning in the fields.

The Example of Seven Daughters

*Exodus 2:16 Now the priest of Midian had **seven daughters**: and they came and drew water, and filled the troughs to water their father's flock.*

From these seven daughters, God provided Moses a wife. Again, God saw fit to include in the Scriptures mention of their willingness to work hard.

A lazy woman is a curse to any man. She is a shameful example to her daughters, and a hindrance to the work of God. Behind the scenes in every successful ministry is a small army of ladies with willing hearts and working hands. This has always been true. Later in the book we will deal with the Bible warnings against slothfulness, but let me say here and now — if you do not develop as part of your character a stellar work ethic, never claim to be a lady.

You do not have to sacrifice modesty or femininity to work hard. If there is a job that needs done that would require you to dress immodestly or to cross-dress, then that is not your job — it is man's work. However, having lived in the country on a small farm these many years, let me testify to the fact that MOST jobs can be done by a lady, while still being a lady. Never use femininity as an excuse for laziness.

Tenet 7

A young lady seeks counsel from her elders, not her peers.

*Titus 2:1-5 But speak thou the things which become sound doctrine: That the aged men be sober, grave, temperate, sound in faith, in charity, in patience. The aged women likewise, that they be in behaviour as becometh holiness, not false accusers, not given to much wine, teachers of good things; That they may teach **the young women** to be sober, to love their husbands, to love their children, To be discreet, chaste, keepers at home, good, obedient to their own husbands, that the word of God be not blasphemed.*

Titus is encouraged to energize the aged women in his congregation to spend time teaching the young women important character traits. This theme is sprinkled throughout the Bible. It is God's plan for youth to learn from the aged and experienced.

Rehoboam was the son of King Solomon. Upon the death of his father, Rehoboam inherited his father's throne, but sadly, not his father's wisdom. He had access to much of that wisdom through both his father's writings and his father's peers. The "old men" who had served with Solomon tried to give him sound and sage advice. This young king forsook their counsel and turned his ears to his peers. These *youths* possessed no greater wisdom than Rehoboam — they were his contemporaries and thus they simply mirrored his knowledge and experience. Yet he chose to follow their untested advice. As a result, a nation was plunged into civil war.

One of the downfalls of young ladies in our society is that many have developed a foolish dedication and arrogant loyalty to their peers. A friend's opinion usually trumps a parent's opinion. What their girlfriends think is more important than what their pastor thinks.

Because of this, unwise decisions have become the norm. No matter how flippant your attitude may have become, you would be wise to remember that poor decisions result in real life, long-ranging consequences. Yes, you may choose what you do, but you do not get to choose the consequences of what you do — they are built-in.

Young lady, your mother knows more than you in most every area of importance. Your grandmother has forgotten more than you presently know! Your pastor and your pastor's wife have special spiritual insight and wisdom. Older, godly women in your church can provide you with a great multitude of counselors. Wise is the young lady who engages regularly with older, wiser women.

Proverbs 20:5 Counsel in the heart of man is like deep water; but a man of understanding will draw it out.

Let me give you a general observation: beware of the one who is quick to give advice. It probably isn't worth much. Wise counsel is like deep water. It exists in the hearts of godly and aged women and if you want to access it, you will have to draw it out.

Learn to treasure the wisdom won by spiritual and practiced experience. Never make a major decision in your life without seeking godly counsel.

Proverbs 15:22 Without counsel purposes are disappointed: but in the multitude of counsellors they are established.

Proverbs 24:6 For by wise counsel thou shalt make thy war: and in multitude of counsellors there is safety.

Proverbs 12:15 The way of a fool is right in his own eyes: but he that hearkeneth unto counsel is wise.

Tenet 8

A young lady is sober-minded.

*Titus 2:3-4 The aged women likewise, that they be in behaviour as becometh holiness, not false accusers, not given to much wine, teachers of good things; That they may teach **the young women** to be sober....*

The word sober has to do with your thinking. The word is defined thus: *to be of sound mind; sane; to discipline and correct your thinking*. Part of what separates immaturity from maturity is mental discipline. If you are going to transition from being a girl into being a lady, you have to put away childish thinking.

*1 Corinthians 13:11 When I was a child, I spake as a child, I understood as a child, **I thought as a child**: but when I became a man, I put away childish things.*

Disciplined Thinking
"...to be sober..."

Let me explain to you how God made you. You are a triune being: body, soul, and spirit. Your flesh is your main problem — it seldom wants to do right. If you are saved, your reborn spirit is your hope! Thank God that when you were saved, you became a new creature in Jesus Christ. So your flesh votes for carnality, your reborn spirit urges spirituality, and the tie-breaker is your soul.

Now, stay with me. Your soul is also a triune being. It consists of your mind, your heart (emotions) and your will. Your mind is the key to everything!   If your thinking is right, your emotions will be right, and your will chooses right. Get these three things right, and your soul is right!   When your soul chooses right, it becomes the tie-breaker between your flesh and your reborn spirit. Reread this paragraph until you fully understand it.

Got it? If you disciplined your mind to stay with me, then you have already come to this conclusion: *the battleground for who you are is won or lost in your mind!*

That is why the Bible has instructed the aged women to teach the young women to be sober-minded. "Sober" means to be self-controlled or disciplined in your thinking.

God has constructed our minds with this blessed characteristic: no human can think of more than one thing at a time! When a young woman understands this, she learns how to eliminate wrong, immature or sinful thinking. To do this, she must be pro-active in choosing what she will think about throughout the day.

Replace daydreaming with diligent thoughts. You can either let your mind drift, or take hold of the reins and steer it.

Psalms 119:113 I hate vain thoughts: but thy law do I love.

Jeremiah 4:14 O Jerusalem, wash thine heart from wickedness, that thou mayest be saved. How long shall thy vain thoughts lodge within thee?

Proverbs 21:5 The thoughts of the diligent tend only to plenteousness;

David, a man after God's own heart, wrote how he hated vain thoughts. Vain means empty, undisciplined or unproductive. Jeremiah the prophet properly points out to the people of Jerusalem that the condition of their wicked hearts (emotions) is because of their undisciplined and unplanned thinking! Proverbs 21:5 gives us the cure: *"The thoughts of the diligent tend only to plenteousness."*

A diligent young lady takes careful oversight of her thoughts. She is not lax. She plans what to think about and carries out that plan.

You will either plan what to think about each day, or you will fall victim to whatever mental fodder this world provides. Your eye gates and ear gates are constantly accosted by evil. The undisciplined, unplanned mind falls easy prey to whatever thoughts and accompanying emotions wander in.

Replace wrong thinking with Bible meditations. The way to win the victory over wicked thinking is through Bible meditation.

Psalms 1:1-3 Blessed is the man that walketh not in the counsel of the ungodly, nor standeth in the way of sinners, nor sitteth in the seat of the scornful. But his delight is in the law of the LORD; and in his law doth he meditate day and night. And he shall be like a tree planted by the rivers of water, that bringeth forth his fruit in his season; his leaf also shall not wither; and whatsoever he doeth shall prosper.

Many of you young ladies have memorized Psalms chapter one. Its verses are so familiar that I am afraid you may have overlooked their promises. Bible meditation is essential to surviving the attacks of the Devil upon your mind. Nothing is more powerful than the Word of God! Jesus defeated Satan's temptations by quoting the Bible. If your mind is assaulted with thoughts of insecurity, envy, jealousy, or depression, then you must discipline your thoughts on the Word of God. Psalms chapter one promises strength, life, fruit, health, and prosperity to the young lady who will do so!

As you spend time each morning reading your Bible, it is essential that you choose out verses to jot down and carry with you throughout the day. Use a 3x5 card. Pull it out when needed and focus your mind on memorizing and meditating on those verses.

Replace worldly thinking with Christ thoughts. The more you study Christ, and meditate on His Word, the more you will acquire His mind.

Philippians 2:5 Let this mind be in you, which was also in Christ Jesus:

Romans 12:1-2 I beseech you therefore, brethren, by the mercies of God, that ye present your bodies a living sacrifice, holy, acceptable unto God, which is your reasonable service. And be not conformed to this world: but be ye transformed by the renewing of your mind, that ye may prove what is that good, and acceptable, and perfect, will of God.

The mind of Christ is characterized in Philippians as one of humility and service — a mind fixed on fulfilling the will of His Father. The worldly mindset is just the opposite. It focuses on self and sin with little regard for eternity. You have to choose how you are going to think about each situation you face today. You can choose a Christ perspective or a worldly perspective. But remember, you win or lose the battle by how you choose! You also decide between maturity and immaturity.

"But I can't help the way I feel!"

Ever heard another woman say this? Ever say it yourself? Guess what? It is not true. Our emotions flow from our thinking — what we think about and how we think about it. Most circumstances can be viewed selfishly or selflessly. The Bible warns us to select carefully what we spend our time thinking upon.

Philippians 4:8 Finally, brethren, whatsoever things are true, whatsoever things are honest, whatsoever things are just, whatsoever things are pure, whatsoever things are lovely, whatsoever things are of good report; if there be any virtue, and if there be any praise, think on these things.

Learn to focus your mental energies on positive things. Everyone of us has something that, if we spend time thinking about, our mind will end up on a dark road. How many times are you going to go down that same road? You know what is at the end of it, right? If there is nothing at the end of that road but depression and despair, refuse to go down it! When you find your mind going to that subject, change roads. Find something constructive and positive to think upon.

Vain thinking, worldly or wicked thinking, self-pity, defeat and despair — put those thoughts away! Through Bible meditation and diligent, positive, Christ-centered thoughts, we can keep our minds focused on things that really matter!

Tenet 9

A young lady is family-focused.

*Titus 2:4-5 That they may teach **the young women** to be sober, to love their husbands, to love their children....obedient to their own husbands, that the word of God be not blasphemed.*

It is vital that a young lady learn the importance of her role in the family unit. Contained in this list of things aged women are to teach young women are three distinct elements of a successful family — three elements that are her God-given responsibility.

Love your husband. The word love in Titus 2:4 speaks of affection. A Christian lady loves her husband and expresses it through true–hearted affection.

Her affection is expressed in many ways: small acts of thoughtfulness, sweet words of love, and simple reminders of her appreciation of all that he does for her. A wise young wife lavishes upon her husband the physical attention that he needs. She does not withhold romance, but instead freely gives herself to her husband.

1 Corinthians 7:1-5 Now concerning the things whereof ye wrote unto me: It is good for a man not to touch a woman. Nevertheless, to avoid fornication, let every man have his own wife, and let every woman have her own husband. Let the husband render unto the wife due benevolence: and likewise also the wife unto the husband. The wife hath not power of her own body, but the husband: and likewise also the husband hath not power of his own body, but the wife. Defraud ye not one the other, except it be with consent for a time, that ye may give yourselves to fasting and prayer; and come together again, that Satan tempt you not for your incontinency.

A young wife who freely and sincerely expresses her affection toward her husband, and faithfully and sincerely gives of herself to his needs safeguards her marriage from evil influences.

A young lady is well taught to remain physically, mentally and emotionally pure during her growing up and courting years. But never forget, once you are married, you are to mentally, physically, spiritually and emotionally, lavish upon your husband unrestrained and unrestricted love!

Hebrews 13:4 Marriage is honourable in all, and the bed undefiled: but whoremongers and adulterers God will judge.

Proverbs 5:18-19 Let thy fountain be blessed: and rejoice with the wife of thy youth. Let her be as the loving hind and pleasant roe; let her breasts satisfy thee at all times; and be thou ravished always with her love.

An enthusiastic love for your *own* husband is and always has been a mark of true femininity. A woman who is cold, distant, uncaring, and unaffectionate toward her husband knows nothing about what it means to be a godly lady.

Love your children. This Bible command encourages young mothers to activate their God-given maternal affection. In a Biblically-structured home, the mother has the chief responsibility to carry out the day-to-day rearing of the children. It may seem strange to some of you that God would instruct aged women to teach young women to love their children, but in this day of "unnatural affection," many young mothers have come to view children as inconvenient and self-restrictive. Bitterness, impatience, and hostility can creep into the heart of a young mother, corrupting the pure maternal love that should flow unhindered from her heart to theirs.

The Bible teaches us and the children's song reminds us that "Jesus loves the little children, all the children of the world." So does a Christian lady! She realizes that their care is a sacred and blessed responsibility. Children are a gift, the Lord's heritage entrusted to each generation.

Psalm 127:3-5 Lo, children are an heritage of the LORD: and the fruit of the womb is his reward. As arrows are in the hand of a mighty man; so are children of the youth. Happy is the man that hath his quiver full of them: they shall not be ashamed, but they shall speak with the enemies in the gate.

As a girl becomes a young lady, she should seek opportunities to work with children. This of course starts in her own home by helping mom with the younger siblings. Never view this opportunity as a task to be resented, but as a training opportunity to be embraced. Babysitting opportunities not only provide practical experience, but also a source of income for a young lady. Volunteering to work in your church nursery and other local church children's ministries will help you develop a true appreciation and wonderful love for God's lambs!

Femininity possesses a grace when interacting with children. Children are always drawn to a Spirit-filled lady, perhaps because their tender hearts sense in that person the love of Christ.

Obey your husband. Liberal feminists have attacked the Scriptural precept of a wife obeying her husband. The modern culture has thrown away almost every Biblical principle for a successful home and marriage. The results have been catastrophic.

The clear , scriptural teaching of the wife living in obedience to her own husband is inarguable. Not only that, the clear warning attached to the teaching should supply sufficient motivation for every Christian lady.

Titus 2:4-5 That they may teach the young women to be sober, to love their husbands, to love their children....obedient to their own husbands, that the word of God be not blasphemed.

Blaspheming the Word of God is not a light thing! To willfully and stubbornly defy the wishes of your husband brings disrespect both to him and the sacred Scriptures. Remember, the husband/bride relationship is compared by God to the relationship between Christ and His church. Submission to your husband's authority should mirror the church's submission to our Savior.

Ephesians 5:22-24 Wives, submit yourselves unto your own husbands, as unto the Lord. For the husband is the head of the wife, even as Christ is the head of the church: and he is the saviour of the body. Therefore as the church is subject unto Christ, so let the wives be to their own husbands in every thing.

(Note: All human authority is limited authority. No one gets to be God but God! That is why the Scripture instructs wives to submit to their own husbands "as unto the Lord" and children to obey their parents "in the Lord." No husband has the right to command his wife to disobey or dishonor the Lord or His Word. If a man does so, he should not condemn his wife for choosing to obey the Lord first and foremost. — Pastor Ross

Acts 5:29 Then Peter and the other apostles answered and said, We ought to obey God rather than men.)

Each young girl transitioning into a young lady should learn from aged women the important part you will have in the family unit. Determine to love both your husband and children, and prepare to dutifully and willingly follow your husband's leadership. Refuse to allow an unscriptural mindset or an ungodly attitude to find root in your heart.

Tenet 10

A young lady is discreet.

*Titus 2:4-5 That they may teach **the young women**...To be discreet...*

What does it mean "to be discreet"?

The word finds its root in two Greek words that together mean: *to save, deliver or protect your feelings, emotions and sensitive nature — to curb, rein in or control your passions or opinions.*

Discretion is self-protection through self-control.

One of the most wonderful things about a young lady is the quality and quantity of your passion. You *feel* things very deeply. God made you this way and it is part of what makes you a delight! It is also something, if not properly disciplined, that can make you an easy target for Satan.

Young lady, you have to guard your heart!

Proverbs 4:23 Keep thy heart with all diligence; for out of it are the issues of life.

Femininity guards itself against manipulation. A young lady must realize that there are those who would take advantage — those who would defraud you by preying upon your emotions. There is many an evil man or carnal friend who, if you are not careful, will use your pure heart and deep feelings to their advantage.

The Five Heart Gates

Every walled city has several gates. No matter how high, sturdy, and thick the walls, if a thief can get through a gate, he can plunder the city. An enticer knows where a young lady's heart gates are! Enticers are master manipulators and they almost always use the same five entry points to stir up your passions, then plunder your purity!

1. Flattery

Proverbs 29:5 A man that flattereth his neighbour spreadeth a net for his feet.

Face it girls, there is not a one of us who does not, at times, battle feelings of insecurity. We often need verbal reinforcement, and appreciate an appropriate and sincere compliment.

Flattery is insincere words. It is a compliment with an ulterior motive. Someone who is constantly lavishing praise upon you very well may be weaving a net with their words. Words are powerful and can be used to evoke strong emotions. They can cause us to overlook obvious character flaws in an individual and let our guard down because "he or she is so nice!"

Once you identify flattery, guard your heart! Whether it is a young man, a peer, or an adult, distance yourself from that person. The pathway of life is littered with the debris of young ladies who believed everything wonderful that people said about them.

2. Pity

An enticer says "Poor you," and we can't help but agree! All of us at times want someone to feel sorry for us. Beware of the person who begins to express pity for you — especially if the words are directed in sympathy toward the supposed limitations of your Christian life.

"I hate it for you that you miss out on so much going to that Christian school."

"It must be hard having such strict parents."

"Wow, I'll bet it stinks having to be in church all the time."

"I feel sorry for anyone who lives in a Christian home. You don't get to do anything fun."

"I can't believe your parents make you dress like that."

If you are not careful, you will soon join them in feeling sorry for yourself. Someone who expresses pity toward you for living for the Lord is not a true friend. Everyone of us ought to be ready to give an answer to those who would wish to manipulate us through false pity.

"I love going to my Christian school and I don't feel like I am missing out on anything."

"I thank God my parents love me enough to have rules for me."

"Church is a blessing! I am not there "all the time," but when I am, I love it!"

"That's funny, because I feel just the opposite — I feel sorry for anyone who is not blessed to be raised a Christian."

"I dress the way I do, not because my parents make me, but because I want to bring glory to God."

1 Peter 3:15 But sanctify the Lord God in your hearts: and be ready always to give an answer to every man that asketh you a reason of the hope that is in you with meekness and fear:

3. Romantic Words

1 Corinthians 13:1 Though I speak with the tongues of men and of angels, and have not charity, I am become as sounding brass, or a tinkling cymbal.

What young lady does not want to hear how beautiful, or how special she is? How exciting it is to have a young man express his interest in or his affection for you. Every young lady has a desire to be loved, and is flattered to think that she has gained the attention of a handsome young man. Such things stir powerful emotions. These emotions, when not guarded, have caused many young ladies to throw away a God-blessed future in exchange for what they later found out was counterfeit love.

The love chapter warns us that angelic, romantic words can be spoken absent of love. History is awash with young ladies who heard "I love you" but failed to understand that it really meant "I lust you!" Promises made are not necessarily promises kept. Many a wicked young man has stolen the purity of a precious young lady who surrendered to romantic words. After he is done with you, that same young man's voice will then resemble sounding brass and tinkling cymbals — annoying, mocking, empty and irritating.

Guard your emotions! Guard your heart! Don't one day weep these words: "But he told me he loved me!"

4. Private Enticement

Psalm 64:2 Hide me from the secret counsel of the wicked; from the insurrection of the workers of iniquity:

Proverbs 9:17 Stolen waters are sweet, and bread eaten in secret is pleasant. **(Words spoken by a tempter!)**

Proverbs 27:5 Open rebuke is better than secret love.

Ecclesiastes 12:14 For God shall bring every work into judgment, with every secret thing, whether it be good, or whether it be evil.

What girl doesn't like a secret? Sometimes it is nice to have something that no one else in the world knows about. From yesterday's fairy tales to today's Hollywood movies, stories of secret love seem to hold us in fascination. However, life is not a children's story or a screen script — life is real!

Please take to heart what I am going to say next: if you have to keep a relationship secret from your parents, then it is not a relationship worth having. Enticers always try to do an end-run around authority. If a young man or anyone else wants to carry on a relationship with you without your parent's knowledge, then their intentions are not honorable. Technology has made it easier than ever before for someone to worm their way into your heart without securing the approval of your parents. Be 100% transparent with your mom and dad about every relationship in your life. This is for your protection.

5. Physical Touch

1 Corinthians 7:1-2 ...It is good for a man not to touch a woman. Nevertheless, to avoid fornication, let every man have his own wife, and let every woman have her own husband.

When it comes to physical touch, strict personal boundaries need to be set in your life. Never underestimate the power of a romantic touch. Women are wired to respond to touch, and carelessness in this area not only breaks down your defenses, but also sends a wrong signal. A polite, proper hand shake is fine, but when a man wants to get more familiar than that, be warned.

Part of being a lady is learning to guard yourself against these five emotional pitfalls. Be wise enough to recognize flattery, avoid pity, and measure the sincerity of romantic words. Be transparent in all of your relationships and guard your personal space. Be discreet!

Tenet 11

A young lady is chaste.

*Titus 2:4-5 That they may teach **the young women** to be....chaste...*

To be "chaste" is to be morally pure. The word comes from the idea of being properly clean; of being innocent and modest. A chaste young lady is a virgin, intent on staying so until marriage. A chaste young wife is loyal to her wedding vows, given only to her husband. Purity before marriage and within the marriage has always been a hallmark of Biblical femininity.

The Example of Christ and the Church

*2 Corinthians 11:1-3 Would to God ye could bear with me a little in my folly: and indeed bear with me. For I am jealous over you with godly jealousy: for I have espoused you to one husband, that I may present you as **a chaste virgin** to Christ. But I fear, lest by any means, as the serpent beguiled Eve through his subtilty, so your minds should be corrupted from the simplicity that is in Christ.*

Paul, writing under divine inspiration, reminds the church of Corinth that they are the espoused bride of Christ. The church is being prepared to be presented to Christ. On the day of His coming, we are to be presented as "a chaste virgin to Christ."

Young lady, chastity is very important to God. The determination of every young lady ought to be to walk down the aisle on your wedding day in a white dress, having never given yourself to any other man — a pure, innocent, virgin bride.

The world has tried to corrupt and cheapen this goal. Our culture has tried to make it acceptable — even preferable — to experiment

45

morally. Virginity is mocked and ridiculed in our culture. Living together before — or as a substitute for — marriage has become the norm. Yet God's opinion has not altered on the subject.

Hebrews 13:4 Marriage is honourable in all, and the bed undefiled: but whoremongers and adulterers God will judge.

Femininity embraces chastity. A godly woman protects her purity. God honors the young lady who dedicates herself to this end. When God was looking for a young lady to carry Christ and deliver Him into this world, God sought out a young virgin. I believe God still reserves special opportunities and special privileges to young ladies who take seriously their chastity.

Honor is not only promised for those who embrace chastity, but judgment is promised to those who undervalue their purity. To willingly sacrifice your virginity on the altar of peer pressure, or in a vain attempt to secure the attention and affections of a young man, is both foolish and costly! God promises judgment as a result of your actions.

Can forgiveness be found? Of course! If we truly confess and forsake sin, God is faithful to forgive. Are there still real life consequences for your actions? Unfortunately, yes. Sometimes those consequences include a damaged reputation, or an incurable sexually-transmitted disease. Many struggle later with guilt, regret, and loss of inner peace. Sometimes impure actions result in the way-too-early responsibility of caring for and rearing a child conceived out of wedlock. Young lady, how much better just to obey God!

No doubt, at some point this chapter will be read by a young lady who, by no fault of your own, had your purity stolen from you. You did not choose it. You are a victim of some type of sexual abuse or assault. Please hear what I am about to tell you — in God's eyes you are as pure and chaste as the day you were born! God's judgment will be directed at the perpetrator, not at you the victim. God loves you, and so do I! Hold your head high, and go forward, dedicated to living a chaste life. Do not let the Devil use this in your life to convince you that your purity no longer matters. God has a wonderful young man waiting for you, and a life you will be blessed to lead.

Tenet 12

A young lady should master the skills necessary to manage a home.

*Titus 2:4 That they may teach **the young women** to be....keepers at home....*

As a lady, you have been assigned by God to be the keeper of your home. That means you are responsible for the success, the organization, the efficiency, and the spirit of your home. This is a great and sacred trust! Home is to be the closest thing to Heaven on this earth, and God placed us as the keepers of this blessed haven. Let's look at the different areas of responsibilities and then recognize the set of skills you must master to properly manage a home.

Self-maintenance and personal growth.

If you are going to be successful at managing your home, you have to first of all take care of yourself! This is not an act of selfishness. If you are not right, it is going to be nearly impossible to see to it that everyone else is all right.

Spiritual maintenance and growth. A time of morning devotions — Bible reading and prayer — is essential. Schedule a quiet few minutes each morning to read from God's Word, and to seek God's face. This will set the tone of your day!

Practical knowledge and encouragement. Yearn to learn! Seek out good books that are informative or inspirational. There are also great audio resources available that can be listened to while chores are accomplished. Be motivated to better yourself through learning.

Psalms, hymns and spiritual songs. Good music ministers to your soul, spirit and body. It brings inner peace and safeguards your home from evil influences. As much as possible, have playing in your home good Christian music.

Physical exercise and a healthy diet. Gals, we need to do our best to take care of our bodies. Spend some time every day exercising. Decide to eat both healthfully and in moderation. This will help you get to your target weight. Once there, weigh yourself often and stay within a ten pound weight window. If you are on the low side, you get to splurge a little! If on the high side, guess what? No food fun for awhile!

Helper and companion to your husband.

Original intent. Remember, we were created to provide help and companionship to our husbands. That is God's plan and purpose for our lives. Hubby is number one! Do whatever is necessary to help him be successful in what God has called him to do.

The magic question. Before he leaves for the day, the best question you can ask him is, "What can I do for you today?" No matter what your plans are, if there is something you can do to save him some time or make his day go better, find the time to do it!

Companionship. Schedule your day around your husband's schedule. No matter what shift he works, make yourself available to him when he gets home from work. The time to run the vacuum cleaner is not when he finally gets home from work and has a few minutes to sit down! Engage him in conversation. Ask him how his day went. Be in a good mood when he comes home! Be engaging and affectionate. Make coming home the best part of his day. Put the children to bed early enough so that you and your husband can enjoy some together time.

Teaching, training and caring for the children.

Put them on a schedule. From newborn to teenager, all children need their mom's help in staying on schedule! Wake-up time, bedtime, play time, study time, work time, nap time, reading time, family time — all should be planned.

Delegating responsibilities. As soon as they are old enough, all children need chores. This will help you around the house, and it will help them to learn diligence and responsibilities.

Creating an environment of peace. Home should be a peaceful place. You accomplish this by establishing and enforcing a code of peacefulness. Here are the rules:

- We don't fight, we get along.
- We talk to each other, we don't yell at each other.
- We encourage each other, we do not put each other down.
- We respect each other's person, possessions, and privacy.
- We pray for each other and pull for each other.

These rules must be modeled before the children in your interactions with your husband. Mom and dad must set the right example. A peaceful, loving, supportive marriage sets the tone for the home.

Fun time! Remember, kids need to be kids! Part of every day should include good, healthy recreation. Get them off the couch, and outdoors. Teach them to use their imaginations and to enjoy simple games. And remember — tired children go to bed early!!!

Cleaning and organizing the home.

Everything in it's place. Organize your living space. Have a place for everything and put everything in its place.

Pack rat! The smaller your home, the more determined you must be to avoid clutter. Don't let things stack up! If you are somewhat of a natural hoarder, you need to learn to throw things away. A cluttered house is impossible to keep tidy and organized.

Efficient, high energy cleaning! At least once a week, you need to give your house a thorough cleaning. Every room should be swept or vacuumed, dusted and uncluttered. Learn to do this quickly and efficiently. Bathrooms should be completely cleaned at least once a week. To make this less daunting, everyday do a quick pick-up. Don't let any room turn into a disaster! A little every day makes cleaning day that much easier.

Meal planning and preparation.

Have a plan! Write out a meal plan each week. This will help you when you go shopping. Buy what you need to fix the 21 meals you will fix in the next 7 days.

Healthful and happy. When you plan your meals, make sure you are feeding your family a well-balanced, healthful diet. Good food can be good for you! Don't turn your kitchen into a special order restaurant. Your children need to learn to eat what is prepared for them.

Family table. Insist on eating most meals together around the dining room table. Meal time is not just eating time! It is a time to interact and catch up on everyone's day. It can also be a great time to read a bit of the Bible together, and pray together.

Shopping!

Make a list. Have a shopping list that hangs somewhere in your kitchen. Mine is on the fridge. As I notice we are getting low on something, I jot it down. These needs, added to our meal planning list, make up our shopping list. Get what you need and beware of impulse buying.

Pinch the pennies. Be willing to clip coupons and compare prices. Check store ads and shop wisely. Buy in larger quantities when it makes sense to do so. Have a budget. Learn to buy the ingredients to make things from "scratch" instead of paying higher prices for less healthful, pre-prepared foods.

Needs and wants. Figure out the difference between what you need and what you want! Learn to say "no" to things that are unnecessary.

Characteristics of a great home keeper.

Schedule. Learning to live by schedule, and training your children to live and stay on schedule is half the battle. Set priorities and schedule a time for each one.

Organization. The best home keepers learn early the importance of organization. A place for everything, and everything in its place. Scheduled time to re-organize your living space each week.

Flexibility. Life doesn't always stay on schedule! There are going to be things come up that throw the best of plans off course. You have to learn to be flexible, and to play catch-up from time to time.

Joy! The ability to do all that you need to do, with joy in your heart and a smile on your face is a gift. Rejoice! If God has given you a husband, children and a home, then you are most blessed.

Tenet 13

A young lady is good.

*Titus 2:4 That they may teach **the young women** to be...good...*

Have you ever said to a friend as you parted company, "Be good!"? Ever have mom or dad say that to you as you left the house? What might seem like a casual parting comment might very well be one of the most important exhortations we can give to one another.

Young lady, "Be good!"

Biblical femininity sets a gold standard of genuine goodness to others. A Christian lady is constantly looking for an opportunity to say or do something good. Read and be challenged by these verses exhorting us to be good, and extend goodness to those around us.

Matthew 5:44 But I say unto you, Love your enemies, bless them that curse you, do good to them that hate you, and pray for them which despitefully use you, and persecute you;

Acts 10:38 How God anointed Jesus of Nazareth with the Holy Ghost and with power: who went about doing good, and healing all that were oppressed of the devil; for God was with him.

Romans 12:21 Be not overcome of evil, but overcome evil with good.

Galatians 6:10 As we have therefore opportunity, let us do good unto all men, especially unto them who are of the household of faith.

Hebrews 13:16 But to do good and to communicate forget not: for with such sacrifices God is well pleased.

1 Peter 3:10-11 For he that will love life, and see good days, let him refrain his tongue from evil, and his lips that they speak no guile: Let him eschew evil, and do good; let him seek peace, and ensue it.

3 John 1:11 Beloved, follow not that which is evil, but that which is good. He that doeth good is of God: but he that doeth evil hath not seen God.

The testimony of Christ is that He "went about doing good." If your ultimate goal is to be like Jesus, then you must do as He did. Every day is filled with opportunities to do good! Leave, in your wake, people touched by God's goodness channeled through you.

Be good to your family. Be a blessing to mom and dad. Contribute to the unity of your family by going out of your way to be good to your siblings. It is hypocrisy to extend goodness in public and evil in private.

Be good to your church family. The Bible encourages us to do good, *"especially unto them who are of the household of faith."* The testimony you should have in your local assembly is one of goodness and grace to all.

Be good to your critics. Christ challenged us to love our enemies and *"do good to them that hate you, and pray for them which despitefully use you, and persecute you."* This very well might be our greatest test! Our carnal nature wants to repay evil with evil. Christian femininity learns to overcome evil with good.

Be good to those in need. People never forget who was there during the hardest times in their life. There is a lot of sorrow and pain in this life. Be especially good to those going through difficult times.

To pass up a chance to do good is a serious thing! As the Holy Spirit guides you through your day, He will bring you opportunities to be a blessing to others. Beware that you do not take lightly these divine appointments!

*Galatians 5:22-23 But the fruit of the Spirit is love, joy, peace, longsuffering, gentleness, **goodness**, faith, Meekness, temperance: against such there is no law.*

James 4:17 Therefore to him that knoweth to do good, and doeth it not, to him it is sin.

Tenet 14

A young lady guards against foolishness.

Matthew 25:1-2 Then shall the kingdom of heaven be likened unto **ten virgins**, *which took their lamps, and went forth to meet the bridegroom. And five of them were wise, and five were foolish.*

There are few things worse than being labeled a fool. The accusation is so severe, so serious, that Jesus gave this warning to his disciples:

Matthew 5:22 But I say unto you, That whosoever is angry with his brother without a cause shall be in danger of the judgment: and whosoever shall say to his brother, Raca, shall be in danger of the council: but whosoever shall say, Thou fool, shall be in danger of hell fire.

Obviously, the word "fool" should not be thrown around carelessly. As a young lady, you need to guard against a reputation of foolishness. The book of Proverbs deals in depth with this subject, and every young lady would be wise to consider each verse that mentions foolishness.

The Bible gives us four specific instances where this unseemly character trait is linked to women.

A young lady is foolish if she is not ready for the return of Christ.

Ten virgins are mentioned in Matthew chapter twenty-five. Of the ten, five were wise and five were foolish. All were morally pure, and all were hanging out together waiting for the coming of the bridegroom. At his coming, five discovered that they did not have oil in their lamps. Five were prepared and went with the bridegroom and five were unprepared and were left behind. This parable is urging us all to make sure that we are truly saved! I fear that many young church girls — many that we would assume are ready for the coming of Christ — will be left behind because they are not really saved. This would be a great time to stop what you are doing and examine yourself carefully. Have you been born again? Are you just playing Christianity, or are you really saved?

Only a fool would let pride get in the way from getting this settled!

A young wife is foolish if she discourages her husband from being faithful to the Lord.

*Job 2:9-10 Then said his wife unto him, Dost thou still retain thine integrity? curse God, and die. But he said unto her, Thou speakest as one of **the foolish women** speaketh. What? shall we receive good at the hand of God, and shall we not receive evil? In all this did not Job sin with his lips.*

Job and his wife were going through a time of intense testing. Few women in history have had to deal with the death of their children, plus the loss of their home, their possessions, and the health of their husband. Remember, all of this happened in a matter of a few days. In her bitterness and heartache, she lashes out at her husband, rebuking him for maintaining his integrity and his loyalty to God. She even tells him to curse God and die!

Her husband rebukes her for speaking "as one of the foolish women." Job had responded up to this point with amazing grace and strength. He was trying his best to be faithful to God! His wife missed a great opportunity to encourage her husband toward God. Instead, she encouraged him to turn his back on God and His divine plan for their lives.

Ladies, life isn't always going to be easy. God's will has as many valleys as mountaintops — and some of those valleys are deep and dark. Biblical femininity finds the strength to encourage a man to great heights and greater service. A true Christian lady stands with her husband and for God during times of great testing.

If I was cruel enough, I could fill the next page with the names of wives who have discouraged their husbands right out of the will of God. I could list the names of men who should be pastoring, but their wives took them out of the ministry. Countless men have surrendered to the mission field, only to have their wives derail God's plan. Scores of laymen should be soul winning, captaining bus routes, teaching Sunday School, preaching in nursing homes — and would be — but for a wife who nagged them into stepping away from serving God. Dear friend, please, I am pleading with you, support your husband as he steps out to serve the Lord! Don't let selfishness or discouragement cause you to speak as one of the foolish women. Encourage his walk with God, and his desire to sacrifice and serve in your local assembly. Stand with him as he stands for the Lord!

A young woman is foolish
who disregards the moral laws of God.

Proverbs 9:13-18 **A foolish woman** *is clamorous: she is simple, and knoweth nothing. For she sitteth at the door of her house, on a seat in the high places of the city, To call passengers who go right on their ways: Whoso is simple, let him turn in hither: and as for him that wanteth understanding, she saith to him, Stolen waters are sweet, and bread eaten in secret is pleasant. But he knoweth not that the dead are there; and that her guests are in the depths of hell.*

What sadness! As I read the description of this "foolish woman," I cannot help but think, "What went wrong?" At one time she was a little girl, and a tender youth. How did she become what we now read? The answer I believe is a simple one — at some point she began to disregard the moral laws of God. And because of this, she now sits on the stoop of her house, offering herself to anyone foolish enough or simple enough to take part in her sin.

There are two basic moral laws that every true lady must honor:

1. Purity before her marriage.
2. Faithfulness to her marriage.

Young lady, you are a fool if you give away your purity to anyone but the man God has for you to marry. Young wife, you are a fool if you give in to the temptation to become unfaithful to your husband. The ripple effect of these selfish and satanic decisions will reverberate to the far-reaching areas of your life. You have contributed to the moral destruction of your nation!

If you have crossed these lines, please, confess them as sin against a holy and righteous God. Commit yourself to a life of purity and faithfulness. God is wonderful in His forgiveness, and the Champion of second chances. But don't play games with Him in this area of your life!

Hebrews 13:4 Marriage is honourable in all, and the bed undefiled: but whoremongers and adulterers God will judge.

A young wife and mother is a fool
when she contributes to the destruction of her home.

*Proverbs 14:1 Every wise woman buildeth her house: but **the foolish** plucketh it down with her hands.*

Many times now, the subject of the home rises to the surface in our study of Biblical femininity. Remember, God created you to be the wife of a very special young man. He has equipped you to bear children, and designed you to anchor your home. If you are wise, you will give yourself to the building of your home. If you are foolish, you will, with your hands, destroy the very things you were created to accomplish.

Do not let the world pressure you into throwing away your original intent. Embrace your femininity and fulfill your calling. A grateful husband and thankful children will one day call you blessed! And a faithful God will reward you both in this life, and in eternity.

Tenet 15

A young lady guards against becoming a busy body.

1 Peter 4:14-15 If ye be reproached for the name of Christ, happy are ye; for the spirit of glory and of God resteth upon you: on their part he is evil spoken of, but on your part he is glorified. But let none of you suffer as a murderer, or as a thief, or as an evildoer, or as **a busybody in other men's matters**.

1 Timothy 5:11-13 But **the younger widows** *refuse: for when they have begun to wax wanton against Christ, they will marry; Having damnation, because they have cast off their first faith. And withal they learn to be idle, wandering about from house to house; and not only idle, but tattlers also and* **busybodies**, *speaking things which they ought not.*

The phrase *busy body* as found in the Bible is properly defined as a person who "works a circuit." Some of you might be familiar with the *circuit-riding preachers* of the 1800s in America. These men worked a circuit by traveling from village to village, town to town, preaching the Gospel of Jesus Christ. A busybody also works a circuit, only they are not spreading the Gospel, but are instead collecting and spreading stories, gossip, and rumors. They collect bits and pieces of information told about other men and other men's business, and whisper what they pretend to know into the ears of anyone willing to listen to their idle gossip.

This may seem a harmless habit. But in the above verses, God lists the sin of being a busy body alongside the acts of murder, thievery, and evildoings. He plainly states that young women engaged in this sorry business are "speaking things which they ought not." How could the Bible be plainer?

Proverbs 26:20-25 Where no wood is, there the fire goeth out: so where there is no talebearer, the strife ceaseth. As coals are to burning coals, and wood to fire; so is a contentious man to kindle strife. The words of a talebearer are as wounds, and they go down into the innermost parts of the belly. Burning lips and a wicked heart are like a potsherd covered with silver dross. He that hateth dissembleth with his lips, and layeth up deceit within him; When he speaketh fair, believe him not: for there are seven abominations in his heart.

Young lady, you must guard against the sin of idle gossip. To spend your life stalking others, pumping people for information, checking social networking sites, eaves-dropping on conversations, and spreading what you find around your community and your church is sinful and shameful!

Gossip is hurtful. It ignites strife and contentions. It seriously and severely wounds innocent people. It reveals things about you that you need to deal with. God says that tale-bearing exposes, to all, that within your heart are seven abominations!

Proverbs 6:16-19 These six things doth the LORD hate: yea, seven are an abomination unto him: A proud look, a lying tongue, and hands that shed innocent blood, An heart that deviseth wicked imaginations, feet that be swift in running to mischief, A false witness that speaketh lies, and he that soweth discord among brethren.

Every gossiper has a problem with pride, and a problem with lying. They delight to shed innocent blood, devise wicked imaginations in their heart, run to mischief and think nothing of being a false witness. To make matters worse, their sin sows discord among God's people.

Are you getting this, young lady? Have you already developed the habit of collecting and spreading idle gossip? I pray that God opens your eyes to the depth of this sin, and brings you to full repentance. Confess and forsake this wicked lifestyle, and use your time, your energies, and your words for the glory of God, and for the good of others.

Tenet 16

A young lady joyfully praises the Lord.

*Psalm 148:12-13 Both young men, and **maidens**; old men, and children: Let them praise the name of the LORD: for his name alone is excellent; his glory is above the earth and heaven.*

Young lady, when was the last time you praised the Lord? God is worthy of our praise. The Bible specifically lists it as one of the responsibilities of young maidens. A real lady understands that God should be constantly and verbally credited for all of the good which He bestows upon each of us.

Many times a day, you should say the words, "Praise the Lord."

Psalms 119:164 Seven times a day do I praise thee because of thy righteous judgments.

Silence in this area is near blasphemy. When you are blessed, or something good falls your way, acknowledge God as the source of that goodness. Never be ashamed to publicly praise the Lord. Do it in front of others. The more you praise the Lord, the more reasons He will give you to praise Him!

Psalms 7:17 I will praise the LORD according to his righteousness: and will sing praise to the name of the LORD most high.

Psalms 21:13 Be thou exalted, LORD, in thine own strength: so will we sing and praise thy power.

Psalms 28:7 The LORD is my strength and my shield; my heart trusted in him, and I am helped: therefore my heart greatly rejoiceth;

and with my song will I praise him.
Psalms 40:3 And he hath put a new song in my mouth, even praise unto our God: many shall see it, and fear, and shall trust in the LORD.

These verses are a mere sampling of those found in Psalms exhorting us to praise the Lord through song. Young ladies should never shy from singing sweetly for the Lord. Sing out during the congregational song service. Join your church choir if you can. Both publicly and privately, sing praises to your God.

A young virgin girl by the name of Mary had a supernatural encounter with God. Her heart was so full that she broke out in spontaneous praise! Read her sweet words and ask God to help you to learn to praise the Lord also.

Luke 1:46-55 And Mary said, My soul doth magnify the Lord, And my spirit hath rejoiced in God my Saviour. For he hath regarded the low estate of his handmaiden: for, behold, from henceforth all generations shall call me blessed. For he that is mighty hath done to me great things; and holy is his name. And his mercy is on them that fear him from generation to generation. He hath shewed strength with his arm; he hath scattered the proud in the imagination of their hearts. He hath put down the mighty from their seats, and exalted them of low degree. He hath filled the hungry with good things; and the rich he hath sent empty away. He hath holpen his servant Israel, in remembrance of his mercy; As he spake to our fathers, to Abraham, and to his seed for ever.

Nothing is more precious than praise. Nothing is more sweetly feminine than when a young lady, with a reborn spirit and a redeemed soul, fully engages in magnifying the Lord. God is worthy to be praised! Throughout each and every day, may you lift up your heart in praise to God.

Tenet 17

A young lady seeks the fullness of the Holy Spirit.

Acts 2:17-18 And it shall come to pass in the last days, saith God, I will pour out of my Spirit upon all flesh: and your sons and your **daughters** *shall prophesy, and your young men shall see visions, and your old men shall dream dreams: And on my servants and on my* **handmaidens** *I will pour out in those days of my Spirit; and they shall prophesy:*

A lady seeks to be filled with the Spirit of God. This filling was promised to the daughters as well as the sons; to the handmaidens as well as the servants. Young lady, God has given you a wonderful gift — the indwelling presence of a member of the triune God. The Holy Spirit indwells every new believer the moment they receive Jesus Christ as Savior. But just because God's Spirit is within you, does not mean that He controls you. Your life has to be yielded to the indwelling Spirit.

The Importance of Being Filled with the Holy Spirit

Being filled with the Spirit is a command of God. It is not optional for the obedient Christian. *Ephesians 5:18 And be not drunk with wine, wherein is excess; but be filled with the Spirit.*

Being filled with the Spirit is so important Christ did not want His disciples to attempt to evangelize without it! Jesus knew that we would not have the divine power, the divine discretion, or the divine direction that we would need in soul winning if we attempted it in the power of our own flesh. *Luke 24:49 And, behold, I send the promise of my Father upon you: but tarry ye in the city of Jerusalem,*

until ye be endued with power from on high.
How to be Filled with the Holy Spirit

One must be emptied in order to be filled. Many of us are so full of ourselves and full of sin, that it gets in the way of complete surrender to the Holy Spirit's control. Every day, we should spend time in genuine confession of our sin and sincere emptying of self. A lady who comes purely and selflessly to God, seeking the fullness of the Holy Spirit, can expect to receive a special anointing of God.

Luke 11:11-13 If a son shall ask bread of any of you that is a father, will he give him a stone? or if he ask a fish, will he for a fish give him a serpent? Or if he shall ask an egg, will he offer him a scorpion? If ye then, being evil, know how to give good gifts unto your children: how much more shall your heavenly Father give the Holy Spirit to them that ask him?

The Fullness of the Holy Spirit Provides A Young Woman the Ingredients Necessary to Be Spiritually Feminine.

Every proper character trait needed is provided through the fruit of the Spirit. Everything we need to be a good wife, a good mother, and a good Christian is provided when we surrender to the control of the Holy Ghost.

Galatians 5:22-25 But the fruit of the Spirit is love, joy, peace, longsuffering, gentleness, goodness, faith, Meekness, temperance: against such there is no law. And they that are Christ's have crucified the flesh with the affections and lusts. If we live in the Spirit, let us also walk in the Spirit.

Do you love people the way you should? Do you have the inner joy, quiet peace, and outward patience needed? Are you as gentle, as good, as meek, and as self-disciplined as you should be? None of us are! That is why we need to be filled with the Holy Spirit.

Both the power and boldness needed to share the Gospel with others is provided when we are filled with the Holy Spirit.

Acts 1:8 But ye shall receive power, after that the Holy Ghost is come upon you: and ye shall be witnesses unto me both in Jerusalem, and in all Judaea, and in Samaria, and unto the uttermost part of the earth.

Acts 4:31 And when they had prayed, the place was shaken where they were assembled together; and they were all filled with the Holy Ghost, and they spake the word of God with boldness.

God has chosen us, His handmaidens, to be a part of the great army of Christians engaged in taking the Gospel to a lost and dying world! To win a soul to Christ is one of the greatest privileges granted to any person. We need Holy Spirit power to boldly witness as effectively as we ought.

Holy Spirit fullness provides us with a joyful spirit, a thankful heart, and a submissive attitude.

Ephesians 5:18-22 And be not drunk with wine, wherein is excess; but be filled with the Spirit; Speaking to yourselves in psalms and hymns and spiritual songs, singing and making melody in your heart to the Lord; Giving thanks always for all things unto God and the Father in the name of our Lord Jesus Christ; Submitting yourselves one to another in the fear of God. Wives, submit yourselves unto your own husbands, as unto the Lord.

When we empty ourselves of self and sin, and seek the fullness of the Spirit, God gives us a song! He puts a melody in our hearts and a smile on our faces. Sin and self always rob a person of inner joy. Holy Spirit fullness brings fullness of joy.

Sin and self also produce an unthankful spirit. Soon we are focused on what we do not have, and blind to our many blessings. The lady filled with the Spirit of God appreciates the people around her, and takes constant note of the goodness of God.

Do you struggle with submissiveness? Self and sin want their way! The Spirit-filled woman honors her husband's position in the home, and joys in helping him carry out his vision for the family.

Holy Spirit fullness protects us from pride, strife, and envy.

Galatians 5:25-26 If we live in the Spirit, let us also walk in the Spirit. Let us not be desirous of vain glory, provoking one another, envying one another.

Many ladies struggle with this triple threat. Honestly, we too often desire vain glory. We want the attention on us and find ourselves fighting for the credit we feel we deserve. Way too often we are drawn into contention with another individual. Many times we struggle with petty jealousy. Dying to self, and confessing these things as sin allows us to let the Holy Spirit take control of our lives. We learn to walk in the Spirit and receive, from Him, humility, peace and contentment.

If we are saved, inside of us dwells the sweet Holy Spirit of God. That just amazes me! I want Him to control me, lead me, guide me, fill me, and use me. I can never be the lady I ought to be without His help. Join me in seeking His fullness and His strength so that we can do what we need to do, and be who we need to be.

Psalm 143:10 Teach me to do thy will; for thou art my God: thy spirit is good; lead me into the land of uprightness.

Romans 8:5 For they that are after the flesh do mind the things of the flesh; but they that are after the Spirit the things of the Spirit.

1 Corinthians 3:16 Know ye not that ye are the temple of God, and that the Spirit of God dwelleth in you?

Ephesians 4:30 And grieve not the holy Spirit of God, whereby ye are sealed unto the day of redemption.

1 Thessalonians 5:19 Quench not the Spirit.

Tenet 18

A young lady is elegantly strong.

*Psalms 144:12 That our sons may be as plants grown up in their youth; that **our daughters** may be as corner stones, polished after the similitude of a palace:*

Proverbs 31:25 Strength and honour are her clothing...

God wished for Israel that their daughters be as "corner stones, polished after the similitude of a palace." The connection between a cornerstone and femininity may not at first reading be apparent. But to those of us who have lived life, borne children, supported our husbands, served the Lord, faced heartache, buried our loved ones, dealt with defeat, experienced victories—while holding together a home—it makes perfect sense.

Young lady, you need to develop an elegant strength. Every palace needs a polished corner stone. And every home needs an elegantly polished, spiritually strong woman.

By definition, the corner stone of any structure provides two vital purposes: it supports the weight of that structure and provides alignment for the walls. The corner stone is what keeps the building steady and straight. Young lady, you need to prepare to be a polished corner stone for your future home.

Strong Constitution

By constitution, I mean your inner make-up. You need to be mentally, emotionally, and spiritually strong. The role of wife and mother requires a tender toughness, and a ton of tenacity!

Ladies, God made us "the weaker vessel" (I Peter 3:7). This makes it even more important that we learn to rely upon Christ and His strength. Life can be hard — sometimes down right brutal! Yet you have (or someday will have) a husband who needs help and companionship, children who need love and nurturing, and a home that needs your attention and oversight. It is vital that we learn to walk with God! The strength to do all that needs to be done is available at the throne of grace. Christ can supply the mental, emotional, and physical strength that you need to do all that He has created you to do.

Strong Convictions

Again, a corner stone is designed to keep the building strong and straight. A woman of strong convictions helps keep her home straight. You need to know what you believe and why you believe it. Young lady, strength is required to implement the Bible principles that define true femininity. Weak, worldly women compromise with the corrupt culture. Surrendering is easier than standing. Shallow silliness takes little effort, but solid spirituality requires strength.

What are your convictions? Are they based solidly on the Word of God? Are you conformed to the world, or have you been transformed by the renewing of your mind? Can someone easily talk you into changing what you believe? Are you "blown about with every wind of doctrine"?

A faithful firmness in what you believe gives security to your children, and provides strong support for your husband. Fickle flakiness provides neither. Develop strong, solid, Scriptural convictions!

Weakness Provides an Opportunity for Strength

2 Corinthians 12:10 Therefore I take pleasure in infirmities, in reproaches, in necessities, in persecutions, in distresses for Christ's sake: for when I am weak, then am I strong.

Nothing is more amazing than experiencing God's strength in our moments of weakness. You may be thinking, "Me, a corner stone?" With the Chief Corner Stone's help, yes! You can develop both a strong constitution and strong, Scriptural convictions.

Philippians 4:13 I can do all things through Christ which strengtheneth me.

Tenet 19

A young lady should strive to be "fair to look upon."

*Genesis 24:15-16   And it came to pass, before he had done speaking, that, behold, Rebekah came out, who was born to Bethuel, son of Milcah, the wife of Nahor, Abraham's brother, with her pitcher upon her shoulder. **And the damsel was very fair to look upon**, a virgin, neither had any man known her: and she went down to the well, and filled her pitcher, and came up.*

*Esther 2:7   And he brought up Hadassah, that is, Esther, his uncle's daughter: for she had neither father nor mother, **and the maid was fair and beautiful**; whom Mordecai, when her father and mother were dead, took for his own daughter.*

*Job 42:15   And in all the land were **no women found so fair** as the daughters of Job:*

*Song of Solomon 1:15   Behold, **thou art fair, my love; behold, thou art fair**; thou hast doves' eyes.*

*Song of Solomon 4:7   **Thou art all fair, my love**; there is no spot in thee.*

*Proverbs 11:22   As a jewel of gold in a swine's snout, so is **a fair woman which is without discretion**.*

A Balanced, Biblical View Point on Outward Appearance

It seems there are two extremes on the subject of a lady's outward appearance. Some ladies are *too consumed* with their appearance while others seem to be *totally unconcerned* with their appearance.

Our culture has definitely placed too much emphasis on outward appearance. We are bombarded with advertisements pushing products that promise to improve our complexions, thin our waists, smooth our hair, and whiten our smiles! We are surrounded in the store check-out aisle by magazine beauties that have been "photo-shopped" and computer-enhanced beyond the boundaries of reality. All of this has left many young ladies feeling inadequate, unattractive, and insecure.

Although we certainly should not get caught up in the world's measure of outward comeliness, the Bible does comment often on the outward appearance of Godly ladies. If this were not important, why would the Lord, by inspiration, make mention of it in His Holy Word? I believe there is a sane, Scriptural balance on this subject of outward appearance. I believe a Christian lady ought to strive to be "fair to look upon."

Femininity Versus Sexuality

There is a clear line of distinction between being outwardly attractive and overtly alluring. Femininity is pleasantly appropriate, while sexuality is purposefully inappropriate! A virtuous lady generates appreciation and respect from men by how she dresses. A strange woman's goal is to defraud and defile the minds of men by how she dresses.

Matthew 5:27-28 Ye have heard that it was said by them of old time, Thou shalt not commit adultery: But I say unto you, That whosoever looketh on a woman to lust after her hath committed adultery with her already in his heart.

A man who looks to lust upon a woman has committed a sin akin to adultery. God holds him responsible for this sin. A woman who dresses to entice from a man a lustful look has also committed a sin. God holds her responsible for dressing to contribute to the sin of heart adultery. Striving to be "fair to look upon" DOES NOT MEAN striving to attract undue and ungodly attention to your body.

Accept What You Cannot Change

Genetics play a role in your basic build and acquired features. There are some things about yourself that you cannot change. You need to accept what you cannot change, and trust the One who created you to be uniquely YOU!

Romans 9:20 Nay but, O man, who art thou that repliest against God? Shall the thing formed say to him that formed it, Why hast thou made me thus?

To harbor bitterness in your heart because of the size of your nose, the shape of your chin, or any other God-fashioned feature is to harbor a secret bitterness toward God. He made you as He chose for His purpose and plan! Accept — no, *embrace* your special uniqueness!

The Great Beauty Equalizer

The most important element of your outward attractiveness is your *countenance*! A young lady's countenance is the effect of her inward spirituality upon her outward features. It is the invisible, yet amazingly visible result of what you truly are on the inside escaping outward! Your countenance is your "God-glow"!

1 Samuel 25:3 Now the name of the man was Nabal; and the name of his wife Abigail: and she was a woman of good understanding, and of a beautiful countenance: but the man was churlish and evil in his doings; and he was of the house of Caleb.

It is not said of Abigail that she was beautiful in her form or features, but rather that she possessed a beautiful countenance. Despite less than ideal circumstances, she maintained an inward spiritual kindness that spilled out beautifully upon her outward visage.

2 Samuel 14:27 And unto Absalom there were born three sons, and one daughter, whose name was Tamar: she was a woman of a fair countenance.

Again, a young lady who was named Tamar is commended in the Scriptures because of her fair or goodly countenance. She may have been plain or striking, we do not know. But her countenance impacted positively her appearance.

How is our countenance enhanced? What does the Bible say about this great beauty equalizer?

Your countenance is affected by inward sin. Unconfessed sin dims your outward glow. *Genesis 4:5 But unto Cain and to his offering he had not respect. And Cain was very wroth, and his countenance fell.*

The best beauty aid in the world is a heart right with God! Don't let sin mar your life. Always respond swiftly to the sweet convicting voice of the Holy Spirit as He reproves you when you fail Him.

Your countenance is affected by inward joy. It is important to keep your heart smiling! Don't take life — or yourself — too seriously. Develop a good sense of humor. *Proverbs 15:13 A merry heart maketh a cheerful countenance: but by sorrow of the heart the spirit is broken.*

You need to determine to find reasons to rejoice. Life is not always fair or easy, yet God tells us to keep a joyful heart. *Philippians 4:4 Rejoice in the Lord alway: and again I say, Rejoice.*

Your countenance is affected by your personal relationship with God. There is a divine anointing that comes upon a young lady who spends time with the Lord. God's presence nourishes her spirit, producing in her a divine glow.

Exodus 34:29-30 And it came to pass, when Moses came down from mount Sinai with the two tables of testimony in Moses' hand, when he came down from the mount, that Moses wist not that the skin of his face shone while he talked with him. And when Aaron and all the children of Israel saw Moses, behold, the skin of his face shone; and they were afraid to come nigh him.

After spending time with God for forty days, Moses came down from the mountain shining! God is light, and spending time in His presence recharges our spiritual batteries. Nothing is sweeter than a young lady who is illuminated by the power and presence of God in her life.

Luke 9:29 And as he (Jesus) prayed, the fashion of his countenance was altered, and his raiment was white and glistering.

The example of our Savior is this — pray and glow! Failing to spend time with God dims the light of your countenance.

Your countenance is affected by the company you keep. Carefully choosing wise companions will improve your character and your countenance. *Proverbs 27:17 Iron sharpeneth iron; so a man sharpeneth the countenance of his friend.*

I have watched girls who possessed a heavenly glow quickly lose it, because of bad company. Show me your friends today, and I will show you what you will be tomorrow. A true friend will bring you closer to God and the wrong friend will pull you away from God.

1 Corinthians 15:33 Be not deceived: evil communications corrupt good manners.

Practical Tips

Your Glory. Long hair is synonymous with femininity. God calls it your glory! It softens your form and frames your features. How long is *long*? A good answer to that question is this: if someone was trying to describe you to another person, and she asked about the length of your hair, would your hair be described as "short," "kind of short," "kind of long," or "long"? A lady stays away from haircuts that in length or style could be considered masculine. Find a hair style that is, for you, both feminine and flattering.

1 Corinthians 11:14-15 Doth not even nature itself teach you, that, if a man have long hair, it is a shame unto him? But if a woman have long hair, it is a glory to her: for her hair is given her for a covering.

Neatness counts. A lady is careful in keeping herself properly presentable. Your clothing should be clean, pressed and mended. Accessories should accent your outfit, not monopolize your appearance. Colors should coordinate, and reflect the proper season of the year. Don't wear hosiery with runs, and wear shoes that are clean and polished.

Fragrance. Smell like a lady! This starts with proper cleanliness and hygiene. Proper use of deodorant and body wash will leave you smelling feminine. Perfume should be used lightly so not to be overpowering.

Form. Genetics have determined that not every woman is going to be a skinny-minnie. Some ladies are built on slightly larger frames than others. That is fine! You should find a body weight that is both healthy and feminine for you. A healthy diet and proper exercise will help you to maintain your target weight. If you need to lose weight, do not starve yourself or use gimmick diets. Cut down on the portions of food you eat, and choose fresh fruits and vegetables over starches and sweets. If you have a considerable amount of weight to lose, consult your doctor and a trained nutritionist, then adopt a healthful lifestyle. You will feel better about yourself, and will be better able to perform your responsibilities.

Make-up. Less is more! Make-up should be lightly applied to accent your features. An over usage of eye shadow or rouge replaces your natural, feminine appearance with a harsh, worldly appearance.

Smile! Nothing will soften and improve your appearance more than a smile that comes from the heart. It will endear you to people and make you feel better about yourself. So, smile!

I placed this chapter on outward appearance near the end of this book on purpose. As I have already stated, I feel the culture has placed undue pressure on young ladies to achieve a look that is impractical and borderline impossible! Don't get caught up in trying to follow the world's standards in this area of your life.

Do work at presenting to the world an appearance that is unquestionably feminine and brings honor and glory to the Lord.

Tenet 20

A young lady is distinctly feminine in her choice of apparel.

Genesis 1:27 So God created man in his own image, in the image of God created he him; **male and female created he them**.

Genesis 5:1-2 This is the book of the generations of Adam. In the day that God created man, in the likeness of God made he him; **Male and female created he them**;

Matthew 19:4 And he answered and said unto them, Have ye not read, that he which made them at the beginning made them **male and female**,

God set a boundary when He created the first two human beings. This boundary is thrice proclaimed in the Scriptures. When He created mankind, He created them male and female. God intended for this boundary to be respected and to remain.

Man was created first by God, formed by His hands from the dust of the earth, divinely gifted a living soul, placed in a garden, and given both responsibilities and rules.

Woman was created second by God, formed by His hands, fashioned around a rib taken out of the man, divinely gifted a living soul, and brought to the man for the purpose of being, for the man, a companion and helper.

God intended for there to be differences between a man and a woman. They were created differently for separate purposes. Their roles are different. Their physical, mental, and emotional make-up is different.

A man is to be masculine. He is to be the leader, provider and protector of his home. He is to love his wife as Christ loved the church.

A woman is to be feminine. She is to be a helper and companion to her husband. She is to be a keeper of the home and the primary caregiver to the children. She is to be in submission to her husband as the church is in submission to Christ.

God set up a boundary between the two genders. The tenets of Biblical masculinity stand in stark contrast to the tenets of Biblical femininity. This is God's plan and God's doing.

The Uni-Sex Movement

Satan has tried to tear down every boundary God has ever established. The Devil has dedicated himself to blending the two genders into one. He has blurred the roles of husband and wife, and has tried to rewrite the purpose of each. Young men are becoming increasingly effeminate and young ladies increasingly masculine. This has resulted in the destruction of the foundation of the family. And since the family is the building block of any successful society, the Devil has made great strides toward destroying our nation.

I explain this because the issue of cross-dressing is a leaf on a much bigger tree. It is the outward manifestation of a culture who has turned their back on the divine intent of their Creator.

Three Principles Governing Our Choice of Apparel

What ladies wear should be unquestionably gender-specific. It should clearly represent our dedication to femininity.

Deuteronomy 22:5 The woman shall not wear that which pertaineth unto a man, neither shall a man put on a woman's garment: for all that do so are abomination unto the LORD thy God.

The clear command from God is that His daughters not wear anything that pertains to a man. We are to keep clear lines of distinction between the genders by how we dress. A lady's dress is to be unquestionably feminine.

Garments that are both traditionally and figuratively tied to masculinity should not be worn by a lady. A garment that is synonymous with authority in the home should not be worn by a lady. God warns that if we cross that line, we become an abomination to Him. I point this out because this is a serious issue with God.

Over a million young men in the United States now occasionally cross-dress. That means they put on women's garments and go out in public. Why is it that we can so clearly see the wrong in a young man walking down the street wearing a woman's garment, but no longer feel the same way when a young lady walks down the street wearing a garment that pertains to men? How did we get here? The church of Jesus Christ surrendered the femininity of our young ladies some fifty years ago, and now we are watching the masculinity of our young men similarly destroyed.

My husband and I have lived long enough to have observed the gender blending of the 1960s lead to the sexual revolution of the 1970s and then the sexual confusion of the 1980s and 90s. Now — at the writing of this book — we have a sitting president publicly calling for the legalization of homosexual marriages. This is where gender blending has led us.

Thank God for a new generation of young ladies who are rededicating themselves to gender-specific dress standards! Many are embracing the modest, feminine apparel that some of their grandmothers surrendered two generations ago.

What ladies wear should be unquestionably modest. Christian ladies understand they are protecting the moral fiber of a nation.

1 Timothy 2:9-10 In like manner also, that women adorn themselves in modest apparel, with shamefacedness and sobriety; not with broided hair, or gold, or pearls, or costly array; But (which becometh women professing godliness) with good works.

A careful, Christian lady not only wants to dress specifically to her gender, but also wants to be modestly covered. Man's concept of modesty and God's concept of modesty have differed from the beginning!

Genesis 3:7 And the eyes of them both were opened, and they knew that they were naked; and they sewed fig leaves together, and made themselves aprons.

Genesis 3:21 Unto Adam also and to his wife did the LORD God make coats of skins, and clothed them.

Adam and Eve's idea of modesty was *aprons*. Notice God replaced their aprons with *coats*, "and clothed them" — leaving us to deduce that God did not see them as "clothed" properly as they were. Seems like mankind has been trying to get its aprons back ever since!

Young lady, dress modestly. Wear dresses and skirts that cover your knee. Bending forward should not reveal any part of your bosom. Stay away from tight, form-hugging clothing. They do not make you look good, they make you look cheap. Shorts are little more than aprons (loincloths). Decide that you are going to be unquestionably modest.

What ladies wear should be unquestionably Christian.

1 John 2:15 Love not the world, neither the things that are in the world. If any man love the world, the love of the Father is not in him.

Stay away from extreme worldly fads. For instance, you might find a garment that is unquestionably feminine and unquestionably modest, but gothic in its design or style. Although it passed the first two tests, it failed this last one.

Be careful not to use your body as a walking billboard for worldly designer labels. Be careful of inappropriate advertisements or designs on your shirts that draw men's eyes where they should not linger. Decide that what you wear will be unquestionably Christian.

How does a lady decide what to wear? She picks out clothes that are *unquestionably* feminine, *unquestionably* modest, and *unquestionably* Christian. It might be time to go through your closet and your dresser drawers. Toss out anything that pertains to a man, exposes too much of your body, is too tight and revealing, or associates you too strongly with this present, wicked culture. A lady only wears that which is, without a doubt, feminine, modest, and distinctly Christian.

Tenet 21

A young lady understands her femininity is vital for the survival of her nation.

*Isaiah 32:9-14 Rise up, ye **women that are at ease**; hear my voice, ye **careless daughters**; give ear unto my speech. Many days and years shall ye be troubled, ye **careless women**: for the vintage shall fail, the gathering shall not come. Tremble, ye women that are at ease; be troubled, ye careless ones...Upon the land of my people shall come up thorns and briers; yea, upon all the houses of joy in the joyous city: Because the palaces shall be forsaken; the multitude of the city shall be left; the forts and towers shall be for dens for ever, a joy of wild asses, a pasture of flocks;*

When God sent Isaiah to pronounce upcoming judgment upon His people, He addresses the *"women that are at ease"* and the *"careless daughters."* God held this group partly responsible for the demise of their nation.

In Romans chapter one, when God describes a culture gone reprobate, He proclaims in verse 27, *"...for **even their women** did change the natural use into that which is against nature."* The wording suggests that God's last line of moral defense — women — had surrendered!

America needs Godly wives and mothers. We need modest, faithful, feminine servants for our local assemblies. If this is going to happen, a generation of young ladies needs to go back to the Bible and choose to embrace its divine definition of femininity.

Please do not be careless with what you have just read! The easiest thing to do is to finish this book, set it down and soon forget the Bible principles it has taught you. Begin now to plan genuine change where it is needed. And thank God daily that He has made you who you are!

Conclusion

Biblical Femininity is achieved by adhering to a code of honor. This code is derived from Bible principles, not from the world's perverse definition of womanhood.

To a Christian lady, this code is sacred. To break this code is to forsake your honor and disappoint your God. Read carefully the code of honor below. It flows from the twenty-one tenets contained in this book. It provides for you a template of Biblical femininity.

For my God, and upon my honor….

….I will choose to be a daughter of God and not a daughter of the world.

….I will embrace the divine purpose of my creation.

….I will begin now to prepare for the young man God has created for me to marry.

….I will firmly reject the character traits of the strange woman.

….I will enthusiastically embrace the attributes of the virtuous woman.

….I will develop a solid work ethic.

….I will seek counsel from my elders, not my peers.

….I will be sober-minded.

…..I will develop a family focus.

....I will be discreet.

....I will preserve my chastity.

....I will master the skills necessary to manage a home.

....I will choose goodness.

....I will guard against foolishness.

....I will guard against becoming a busy body.

....I will joyfully praise the Lord.

....I will seek the fullness of the Holy Spirit.

....I will ask Christ for elegant strength.

....I will strive to be "fair to look upon."

....I will choose apparel that is unquestionably gender-specific, unquestionably modest, and unquestionably Christian.

....I will help preserve my nation by providing the salt and light of Biblical femininity.

If you choose to enter into this sacred covenant with God, the line provided above is for your signature. This should be done privately, prayerfully and sincerely.

May God bless you as you strive to be your very best for Him!

About the Authors

With the writing of this book, Jerry and Sheryl Ross celebrate thirty-two years of working with young people. Pastor Ross is the senior pastor of the Blessed Hope Baptist Church, in Jasonville, Indiana, an author, and Bible conference speaker. His wife, Sheryl, is her husband's personal secretary as well as secretary for both their church and their Christian school. In addition to being a homemaker and grandmother, she also oversees their publications ministry.

Other Titles by Pastor Jerry Ross
The Teenage Years of Jesus Christ
Stay in the Castle
The Seven Royal Laws of Courtship
Is Your Youth Group Dead or Alive?
Grace Will Lead Me Home
The 21 Tenets of Biblical Masculinity
The 21 Tenets of Biblical Femininity (by Jerry & Sheryl Ross)

Coming soon by the author:
The Childhood Years of Jesus Christ
104 Teen Training Hour Lessons — Vol. 1
104 MORE Teen Training Hour Lessons — Vol. 2

Ultimate Goal Publications
4969 West County Road 1200 South
Jasonville, Indiana 47438

Order by phone: (812) 665-4375